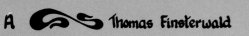 A Thomas Finsterwald   Finsterwald Art Glass   Santa Cruz, Ca.

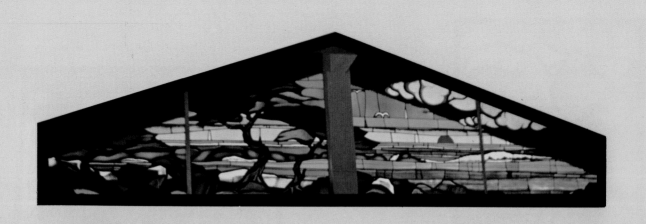

B   Robert W. Hill   Hill/Brusey Stained Glass Studio   Soquel, Ca.

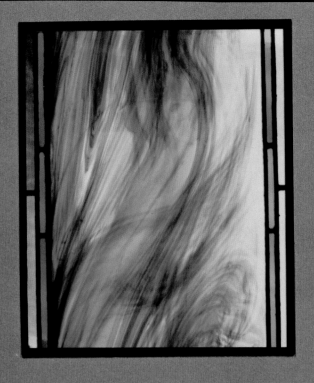

Luciano Palo Alto, Ca.

D 〜〜〜 Jos Maes   Jos Maes Stained Glass   Laguna, Ca. 〜〜〜

 Skip Willis   Lanier Glass   Wash. D.C.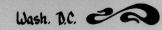

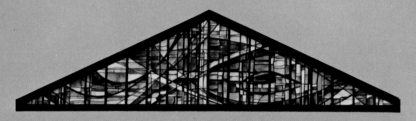

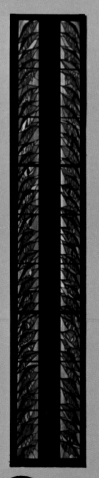

F Jos Maes   Jos Maes Stained Glass   Laguna, Ca.
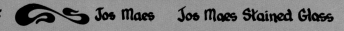

6 Peter Mollica   Mollica Stained Glass Berkeley, Ca.

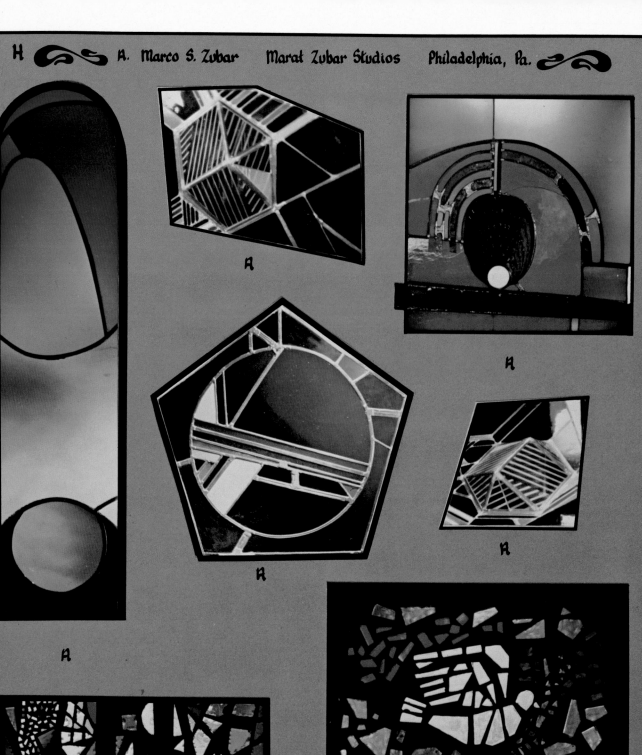

A

A

A

A

A

B

B

STAINED GLASS WINDOW ART

by
Luciano

Revised Edition

Hidden House Publications
Palo Alto, CA

ACKNOWLEDGEMENTS

The author gives a large "thank you" to the following people for their professional assistance and personal support:

George E. Schattle . . Art Direction and Production Supervision
Kristi Carlson . . . . Illustrations
Barbara Smith . . . . Line Art
Judy Whitaker Bishop . . . . Editing
Chuck Koehler . . . . Cover Photography
Robert W. Hill . . . . Technical Review
Cathy Duncan . . . . Assistant to the Author

The author also thanks the many designers and studios for their significant contributions of designs and windows. They are identified throughout the book where their work appears.

DISTRIBUTION

TO BOOK STORES

Quick Fox, Inc.
33 West 60th St.
New York, NY 10023
(212) 246-0325

TO ALL OTHERS

Craft Trends, Inc.
2698 Marine Way
Mountain View, CA 94043
(415) 961-2033

Table of Contents

Section	Description	Page
	Note to the Reader	4
1	Stained Glass Window Making Process	5
2	Designing For Window Art	6
3	Cutline Drawings and Lay Out	9
4	Pattern Making	14
5	Stained Glass Section	16
6	Glass Cutting	19
7	Leading	24
8	Soldering	29
9	Cementing	31
10	Final Treatment and Window Cleanup	33
11	Window Installation	35
12	Copper Foil Technique	37
13	Stained Glass Tools	40
14	Stained Glass Work Area	42
15	Glossary of Terms	44
16	Available Window Pattern	46
17	Designs of Old	47
18	Contemporary Window Art	62
19	Project Windows	85
20	Project Cutline Drawings (fold out)	96
21	Appendix: A visual introduction to the variable and extensive beauty of stained glass, with brief discussions of the glass-making techniques.	

A NOTE TO THE READER

Stained Glass Window Art is enjoying a resurgence and the magic of this eleventh century craft is drawing an ever increasing universe of both craft people and initiates. As this is a project-oriented book, no extensive discussion of the evolution of stained glass window art is presented; nor is this book intended as a technical encyclopedia of the required craft skills. However, you will find in this book:

(1) a general introduction to the craft of making stained glass art windows.
(2) step-by-step instructions applicable to the designs and construction of a stained glass art window.
(3) two cutline window designs (full-sized patterns) which may be removed from the book and used directly for a project.
(4) reproductions of more than 100 traditional window art designs, some of which date back several centuries.
(5) more than 125 contemporary window art designs representing the work of twenty present-day stained glass artists from studios across the country.
(6) an appendix which presents a visual introduction to the variable and extensive beauty of stained glass, with brief discussions of the different glass making techniques.

I feel this book will be of particular use to the beginning craftsperson. If you intend to enroll in a stained glass class, this book will ably serve as your project oriented textbook. Once you have obtained the needed technical skills, you may find the traditional and contemporary designs presented in this book to be a stimulating source of future window ideas.

I hope the accomplished craftsperson will find this book a worthwhile addition to his library and a source of useful technical suggestions and design ideas.

I wish you all good cutting!

Section 1
Stained Glass Window Making Process

The following steps, presented in work sequence, describe the processes by which an idea is transformed from a mental vision into the beauty of a stained glass window. Each of the steps below is discussed in detail in the sections that follow.

WINDOW DESIGNING This is the act of physically representing an idea and/or feeling by combining the elements of line, space, color, and texture within the media of glass and lead.

CUTLINE DRAWINGS AND LAYOUT A cutline drawing or cartoon is the full-sized black and white drawing made to the size of the desired finished window. Layout is the technical translation (i.e., exact measurement) of the design needed to fit the window to an existing opening, such as a window frame.

PATTERN MAKING A pattern or template is made of heavy paper stock (such as mechanics pattern paper) for each section of glass within the window design. The patterns are then used to guide the cutter in scoring a piece of glass to the exact size and shape of each section within the cartoon.

STAINED GLASS SELECTION Choose your stained glass for reasons of both the color *and* texture that best expresses the design concept.

GLASS CUTTING This is the act of scoring a piece of glass with a stylus containing a sharpened hard steel wheel or a diamond chip in its working end, and then pulling away the excess glass to obtain the desired shape and size of the glass section(s) to be used in the window.

LEADING OR GLAZING This is the process for assembling the cut glass sections using channeled lead came to hold the glass sections in place.

SOLDERING Once the window has been "leaded-up," it is necessary to use solder to join the areas, commonly referred to as *joints,* where the lead channels intersect.

CEMENTING This is the application of a caulking compound to the soldered window in order to make it waterproof and tighten the glass within the lead channels.

FINAL TREATMENT OF THE LEAD AND SOLDER Various techniques may be used to darken or color the solder and lead and to texturize the surface of the lead.

WINDOW CLEANUP Prior to installing the completed window, the glass is cleaned and polished.

WINDOW INSTALLATION This is the process of installing the leaded window into an existing frame.

The steps discussed above are based on the leaded stained glass window technique. Section 12 in this book discusses the copper foil technique of window assembly as an alternative to leading.

Section 2
Designing for Window Art

This section presents preliminary guidelines for developing your own window designs.

FIRST   Read thoroughly and completely the total process for transforming a concept into a completed stained glass window. (Sections 1 through 15 in this book)

SECOND   Become familiar with *both* the range of possibilities *and* the technical limitations of glass.

THIRD   Do not rush through the design phase. A good design may require several days of incubation and execution.

FOURTH   Remember that design excitement is more important than technical competence.

FIFTH   Study all art media to stimulate ideas of form, color, and composition.

The four major design elements to consider are (1) composition (2) color (3) texture (4) leadlines.

INITIAL DESIGN PROCEDURE
Begin the design process by listing the following:

Limitations—window size and shape; subject alternatives; light source; type of architecture; room color scheme; availability of glass; budget limits (finished windows may run $4 to $5 sq. ft. for materials)

Needs—bold or delicate design; horizontal or vertical feeling (emphasis); cool or warm color scheme; type of architectural motif

After listing the above criteria, review art books, paintings, photographs, magazines, and design books for compositional ideas.

SKETCHING
1. Begin with "doodles" and thumbnail sketches.
2. Follow with bold conceptual sketches.
3. Reinforce and expand favorable lines; reject others.
4. Repeat this incubation process until a theme and representative lines take hold.

ADDING COLOR WASHES (with watercolors)
1. Use pale yellow to represent warm tones.
2. Use pale blue to represent cool tones.
3. Begin adding additional colors, building a "color feeling" as you go through this trial and error process.

6

ADDING LEAD LINES
1. Let the bleed area of paint suggest lead lines.
2. Give consideration to the limitations of certain types of glass cuts.
3. As the pattern of lead lines develops, make them more dominant by using a felt pen or black crayon.
4. Lead came is available in many widths and shapes—use these to add emphasis and impact to the design.

TRADITIONAL DESIGN APPROACH
1. Begin with lead line drawings and then make overlays on tracing paper, going through several revisions until the design feels right.
2. Then add color using the warm and cool technique. (Traditionally, color is the most important factor.)

TRADITIONAL DECORATIVE COMPOSITION (See Section 17.)
1. The focal interest of the window (the medallion) is usually done in primary colors—reds, yellows, and blues.
2. The background areas (called the field) surrounding the medallion should be comprised of pale tones.
3. Typically, the design is symmetrically balanced.
4. Borders should not have greater impact than the medallion or they will detract from the design.

CREATIVE CONTEMPORARY COMPOSITION (See Section 18.)
Contrast is the primary factor in successful contemporary composition. The objectives of contrast are applied to:

SHAPES contrast large with small, rounded with linear.
LINES contrast thick with thin, bold/simple with detail.
GLASS contrast smooth with texture, opalescent with antique, clear with color, color with mirror, etc.
COLOR contrast warm with cool, pale tones with deep, brights with neutrals and greys

Further, there is a sense of contrast among the four elements of shape, line, glass, and color.

COLOR FACTORS (See Section 5.)
1. Warm colors advance and are generally exciting.
2. Cool colors recede and are generally restful.
3. Neutrals create another visual dimension and increase the importance of both color and lead lines.
4. Strong color itself does not guarantee a good design.
5. Stained glass colors change in artificial light.
6. Glass color can change when positioned next to another color. This is due to the *halation effect.*

EVALUATION OF FINAL DESIGN
Look at your design and ask yourself two questions:
1. Can the color stand alone without the necessity of lead lines? (Does the design work on the basis of color alone?)

2. Can the lead lines stand alone without the necessity of color? (Does the design work without any color?)

If both answers are *yes,* your design is probably good. Finally, if the design "feels good," then begin the preparations for making your first stained glass window.

FINAL CONSIDERATIONS

1. Limit your first project to a window that is no more than 4 to 5 square feet in area.
2. Do not make a practice window. Develop a good design for your first project and execute it with a full commitment to use the window in your home.
3. The maximum recommended glass panel size is 8 square feet, and the maximum recommended size of one dimension is 4 feet.
4. The completed panel will weigh approximately 4 pounds per square foot when completed.
5. Before completing your first design, review the design constraints noted in Section 6 (Glass Cutting) and Section 7 (Leading).

Section 3
Cutline Drawings and Lay Out

This section presents the techniques for developing the full-sized drawing to be used as the "engineering plan" for your window. The steps involved include:
1. Drawing a sketch—the first creative step.
2. Sizing the window and determining the window dimension.
3. Developing a drawing—the final sketch drawn on grid paper.
4. Developing a cutline drawing—the full-sized drawing which will serve as the assembly guide as well as the cutline guide for patterns.

RECOMMENDED TOOLS AND MATERIALS
(1) sketching pad—plain paper 8½" × 11"
(2) graph ruled paper—¼" squares, 8½" × 11"
(3) carbon paper
(4) hard [4H] pencil
(5) felt tip pen
(6) scotch tape
(7) thumbtacks or push pins
(8) vellum
(9) butcher paper—at least 30 pound weight
(10) yardstick
(11) T square (optional)
(12) right angle guide

THE SKETCH
Follow the procedure presented in Section 2 for the development of the final sketch. When you have completed the sketch, the next required step is to size the window.

SIZING THE WINDOW
If there is an existing window you wish to replace with the stained glass window, exact measurements need to be taken. This can be done in the following manner:
1. Measure the *width* of the window top and window bottom. Then take two additional *width* measurements about ⅓ and ⅔ up the window sides.
2. Measure the *length* of each vertical side of the window.
3. In steps 1 and 2 your measurements are of the daylight area. (See Figure 1.)
4. If you can visibly determine how far the existing window sets in the sash, add that measurement to your daylight dimensions. If you can't easily determine the amount of inset, add ¼" to all four sides of the daylight dimensions. (Figure 2.)
5. If you can determine the amount of inset, for example, 5/8" into the sash on all four sides, subtract 1/8" from 5/8" and then add the remaining ½" to all four daylight sides. The 1/8" reduction gives you some breathing room when installing the leaded window.

If you are not making a leaded window to replace an existing window, it is recommended that your first effort be restricted in size to about four square feet (2' × 2' or 20" × 28"). (See Section 11 for discussion of sashes.)

1. Daylight Area of Existing Window

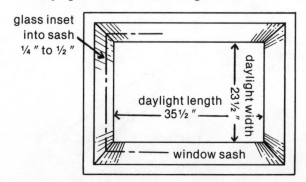

glass inset into sash ¼" to ½"

daylight length 35½"

daylight width 23½"

window sash

2. Daylight Dimensions Expanded to Full-Sized Perimeter Lines

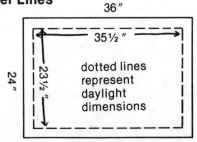

36"

35½"

24"

23½"

dotted lines represent daylight dimensions

solid lines at 24" × 36" are the full-size perimeter lines

SCALED DRAWING

Once you have determined the window dimensions, you are ready to make the scaled drawing.

1. Take the graph ruled paper of ¼″ squares and, using 3″ on the graph paper to one foot of window size, draw the full-sized, perimeter lines. For example, if the window is to be 2′ × 3′, draw a rectangle 6″ × 9″ on the graph paper. Draw moderately heavy vertical and horizontal lines every 1″ (or 4 squares) through the rectangle. (See Figure 3.)
2. Using your sketch as a guide, lightly draw your design on the graph paper within the gridded rectangle. Then, when complete, darken the design lines. (See Figure 4.)
3. Be certain that your drawing is square at all the corners (unless the existing window is not square). You are now ready to make the full-sized cutline drawing (cartoon).

3. Scaled Drawing on Graph Paper

3″ to 1′ scale
guide lines every 1″

9″
equals 3′

6″
equals 2′

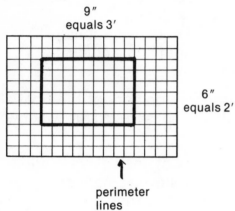

perimeter
lines

4. Window Design Drawn Over Scaled and Gridded Perimeter Outline

9″

6″

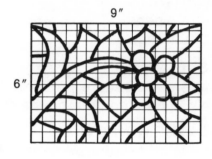

DRAWING THE FULL-SIZED CUTLINE DRAWING (cartoon)

1. Take a sheet of at least 30 pound butcher paper or vellum that is 4″ wider and 4″ longer than the perimeter window dimensions and tack or tape it to your surface drawing.
2. The next step is to arrive at the cut lines or glass cutting size for the window.
3. This means you must account for the perimeter lead which will go around the glass area. Usually you will use 5/8″ or 3/8″ lead. The dimensions 5/8″ and 3/8″ refer to the width of the lead leaf (crown). Generally, the heart of lead came is 1/16″ thick regardless of the leaf width. (See Figure 5.)

5. Lead Channel ("H" round)

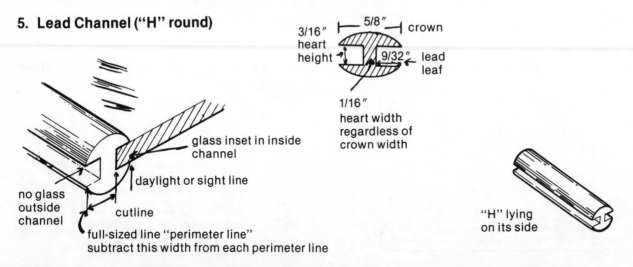

3/16″
heart
height

5/8″ crown

9/32″ lead leaf

1/16″
heart width
regardless of
crown width

glass inset in inside channel

daylight or sight line

no glass
outside
channel

cutline

full-sized line "perimeter line"
subtract this width from each perimeter line

"H" lying
on its side

10

4. The outside edge of the lead cannot extend past the full-sized perimeter lines or the finished window will be over-sized and not fit the opening.
5. The cut lines for the glass nearest the perimeter lines (full-sized) must be in from the full-sized perimeter lines by the width between the outer edge of the lead and the side of the lead heart next to the glass. (See Figure 6.)
6. Check your measurements twice; then draw in the cut lines on the butcher paper. Check that all the lines are square. Read the above steps several times until you clearly understand the concept and the requirements for getting an accurate full-sized drawing with the appropriate cut lines. If your cut lines are not accurate, you will pay the dues when you attempt to install the window.

6. Full-Sized Drawing

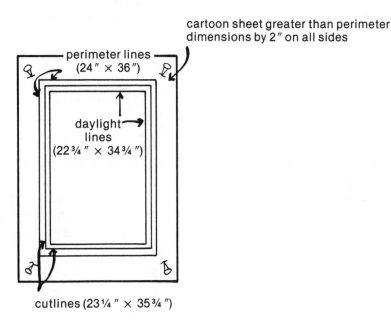

cartoon sheet greater than perimeter dimensions by 2″ on all sides

perimeter lines
(24″ × 36″)

daylight lines
(22¾″ × 34¾″)

cutlines (23¼″ × 35¾″)

HOW TO SCALE-UP THE WINDOW DESIGN TO FULL SIZE

1. Once you have the full-sized perimeter and cut lines on the butcher or cartoon paper, measure off a 1″ grid along the horizontal and vertical axis (perimeter lines). Connect the points with a hard pencil to form a cartoon grid of 1″ squares. Every 4″ draw a heavier line. (See Figure 7.)
2. It is now quite simple to use your scaled drawing (6″ × 9″ in our example) to locate and proportion your design on the full-sized cartoon.
3. After completing the single cutline design, you must now go back and add a parallel line 1/16″ from each single line to provide the space for the lead heart. (See Figure 8 and Section 7.)

7. Gridding the Cartoon and Scaling-Up the Design

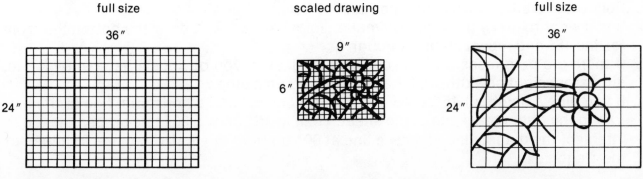

full size	scaled drawing	full size

36″   9″   36″

24″   6″   24″

11

8. Drawing the Internal Cutlines

1. single lines for cuts

completed single line design

2. draw parallel lines 1/16″ from single lines

3. fill space with felt tip pen

4. You can fill in the lead heart space with a medium tip soft felt pen so that your cut lines are strongly visible.

5. Place a sheet of vellum over the full-sized cartoon and trace the cutline drawing. This copy is back up in case the primary cartoon is damaged or lost. It can also be used for glass cutting to shape, using the English technique described in Section 4.

You have now completed the process for developing the "engineering plan" of your window design.

METHOD TO SIZE AND PROPORTION THE WINDOW FROM EXISTING DESIGN WITH GIVEN DIMENSIONS

Here is an easy technique for scaling-up any design concept contained in this book to a given size, while maintaining the sizing proportions shown. Let's use the project window shown on page 86, which was done by the designer in a 21″ × 18″ size. You would like to increase it to 24″ wide and you need to determine how high it should be.

1. Take a sheet of paper 30″ wide (at least 4″ more than the window width) and probably 24″ long (an estimate).

2. Tack it down and center a line 24″ long at the bottom of the sheet.

3. Use a right angle and at the left corner of the line draw a vertical line up the sheet nearly to the top.

4. Place the design (traced from the book) in the bottom left hand corner, lining up the design lines, left vertical and bottom, with the perimeter lines of the cartoon.

5. Follow the steps shown in figures 9 and 10 below.

6. If you want to make the window smaller, let's say 18″ × ?, draw the bottom horizontal line 18″ and repeat steps 3 through 5.

7. If there are no dimensions on your chosen design, you obviously have to pick one, either for height or width, and then follow the same steps.

8. If you pick a height of 15″, draw the left vertical 15″ and a horizontal line at the bottom to the right hand edge of the sheet. Then at 15″ draw a 90° line across the top to intersect the diagonal; and draw a line at 90° up from the horizontal line to intersect the diagonal.

METHOD TO SCALE UP A WINDOW DESIGN

9. Cut Line Layout

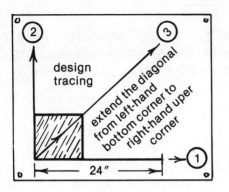

design
tracing

extend the diagonal
from left-hand
bottom corner to
right-hand uper
corner

24″

10. Cut Line Layout

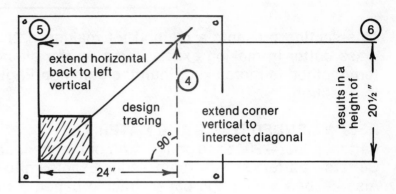

extend horizontal
back to left
vertical

design
tracing

90°

24″

extend corner
vertical to
intersect diagonal

results in a
height of
20½″

Section 4
Pattern Making

This section presents a method for making patterns (templates) used to guide your glass cutter in making exact scores on the glass to fit the shape desired. This pattern method is more exact than the common English method discussed at the end of this section.

RECOMMENDED TOOLS AND MATERIALS
Pattern paper—90 to 110 pound Kraft or butcher paper
Cutters—pattern shears, double edge Exacto knife or two razor blades
Also needed are carbon paper, tracing paper, a fine tip ball point pen or hard pencil (4H) and scotch tape.

PREPARATION (See Figure 1.)
1. Place Kraft paper down first. Pattern sheet should be at least as large as the cutline drawing. (See Section 3.)
2. Lay out enough carbon paper sheets to cover pattern paper.
3. Place cutline drawing over carbon sheets.
4. Use thumbtacks or map pins at the 4 corners of the cutline drawing.
5. Number all the pieces on the cutline drawing, using a ball point pen or hard pencil.
6. Be careful to stay on the cut lines and trace the complete design. For the window perimeter lines and all long straight lines, use a straight edge to guide your pen or pencil.

TO OBTAIN PATTERNS
1. Remove the cutline drawing and carbon sheets.
2. Carefully cut out each pattern, using one of the recommended tools shown in Figure 2.
3. It is important that you keep the cutting tool accurately over the cut lines representing the lead heart.

1. To Draw Patterns

1/16″ lead heartspace

A. is the full-sized cutline drawing

B. is the carbon paper

C. is the pattern paper

Use thumbtacks to hold all three sheets in place.

14

When all the patterns are cut out, place them back on the cutline drawing and check for accuracy. Retrim or even redraw and recut a specific pattern if the cutting is inaccurate. If one particular pattern, such as a border piece, is repetitive, cut several duplicate patterns, as the edges of the pattern will get frayed with multiple use.

TRANSPARENCY METHOD

This English method does not use patterns but places the glass to be cut over the cutline drawing and then scores the glass free hand without using a pattern (template guide). This requires a great deal more glass cutting skill to achieve the accuracy of pattern guided cutting. Further, if the glass is not transparent or is very dark, a light table is needed to show the design image through the glass. (See references in sections 6 and 15.)

2. Alternate Cutting Tools

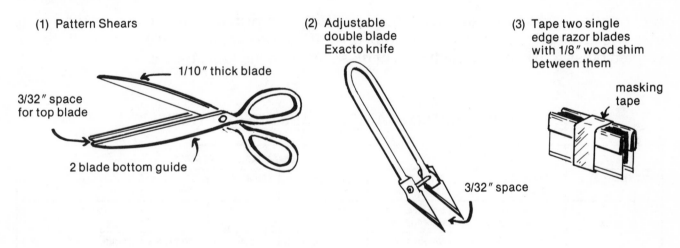

(1) Pattern Shears

1/10″ thick blade

3/32″ space for top blade

2 blade bottom guide

(2) Adjustable double blade Exacto knife

3/32″ space

(3) Tape two single edge razor blades with 1/8″ wood shim between them

masking tape

3. To cut patterns out from Kraft paper drawing

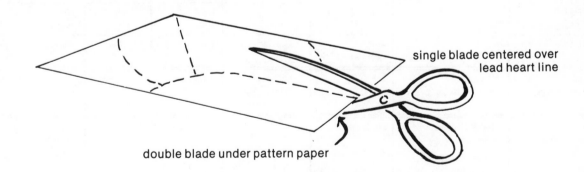

single blade centered over lead heart line

double blade under pattern paper

Section 5
Stained Glass Selection

The selection of glass for your window is a most demanding task, as the effect of the chosen glass will dominate your presentation. In selecting the glass, there are at least four factors to consider:
1. color or colors (some glass is multi-colored)
2. texture
3. degree of transparency
4. thickness

A good way to discover and subsequently "feel" the differences among all the types of glass available is to visit a studio or craft store which handles retail sales of stained glass and examine each type of glass listed in the table below.

GENERALIZED STAINED GLASS DESCRIPTIONS

GLASS TYPE		MANUFACTURING ORIGIN	CHARACTERISTICS OF GLASS				
			DEGREE OF TRANSPARENCY	TEXTURE	COLOR RANGE	GENERAL THICKNESS	CUTTING EASE
ANTIQUE handblown glass		England, France, Germany, et/al.	High transparency to low translucence				From dependable to difficult
	Clear		Highest	Clear with crystal-like striations	Hundreds	1/8″ to 1/4″	Consistently the most dependable
	Seedy		Highest to cloudy	Internal bubbles	50 to 75	1/8″ to 1/4″	Same as above
	Streaky		Varied	Typically clear	Multi-colored variations	3/16″ to 3/8″	Tends to be difficult
	Flashed		Usually High	Clear	Limited	3/16″ to 3/8″	Fairly to very difficult
	Krackle		Nearly transparent	Like cracked ice	3 to 4	1/8″ to 1/4″	Fairly easy
BLENKO Am. handblown glass		Made by Blenko Glass Co.	High to translucent	One heavily Textured ripple	At least 100	1/8″ to 3/8″	Thin end of sheet cuts easily; thicker end is more difficult.
CATHEDRAL machine rolled glass		Made by 3 domestic companies: Kokomo Opalescent Glass Co. Wissmach Glass Co. Hollander Glass Co.	High to Opaque				From very easy to very difficult
	Clear		High but not as high as antique	Heavy regular texture	Hundreds	1/8″	Ranges from very easy to more difficult
	Marine Antique		Same as above	Same as above	Same as above	1/8″	Same as above
	Granite Backed		Translucent	Heavy texture	Limited	1/8″	Same as above
	Hammered & Flemish		Translucent	Heavy texture	Limited	1/8″	Easy to moderately difficult
	Streaky		Usually dark translucence	Heavy regular texture	Limited	1/8″	Same as above
	Opalescent		Translucent	Same as above	Limited	1/8″	Easy to difficult

"Antique" glass is the term which describes imported handblown glass. "Cathedral" glass refers to machine-rolled glass made in the United States. "Flashed" glass is a layer of colored glass fused to another piece of colored or plain glass. "Rondels" are round pieces of glass with a swirl in the middle. "Opalescent" glass is an opaque, cathedral-like glass usually containing at least two streaked colors and having an overall milky appearance.

GLASS SELECTION CONSIDERATIONS

Color is typically the primary selection consideration. In stained glass, color is "alive"—that is, it will tend to blend with colors adjacent to it, crossing over the lead line by a process known as "halation." Depending upon placement, the color may spread to another color or recede from it.

SEVERAL COLOR SELECTION GUIDES ARE:

1. When possible, always look at the prospective glass in daylight and in direct sunlight. Glass undergoes changes in artificial light.
2. Place the several colors chosen next to each other on a windowsill and feel their combined effect.
3. Blues and ambers are good background colors.
4. Reds, particularly brilliant reds and ruby, are very dominant colors and can be overwhelming when used excessively. Orange is also very dominating.
5. White (opaque) glass is used to tone down the impact of abutting glass of dominant tones.
6. Softer tones of yellow are more pleasing than the very brilliant yellows.
7. Greens have a very high degree of compatibility with many colors.
8. Do not overlook the stained glass "greys" which tone down or subdue bright colors. Some examples are blue-grey, green-grey, salmon-grey. Used properly, surrounding the high interest area in a window, these grey tones tend to 'push" the theme to the forefront.

There is also a glass available called "variegated" in which the density and color tone vary, due to a method of color mixing and the varying thickness of the sheet itself.

Under certain design considerations, common door and bathroom window glass can be both interesting and attractive.

TEXTURES

The textures available in stained glass should be used for variety as well as emphasis of the design within the window.

THICKNESS

The varying thicknesses within one sheet of glass can be useful for obtaining gradual changes in color tone—such as for sky or fields. The thicker portion of the sheet is more difficult to work with than the thinner. If the glass is too thick, it won't fit in the standard lead heart height and higher heart came is then used. ("Blenko" lead)

TRANSPARENCY

Use the more transparent glass where little direct sunlight is available. Use the more opalescent glass where privacy is desired or when you do not want the outside view to be visible.

AMOUNT OF GLASS

1. Generally, buy at least 25 to 30% more glass than needed to cover the design area (i.e., 30% more than the square inch area).
2. If the design area has many large curved shapes, buy at least 50% more glass than the area to be covered.
3. There is less waste in cutting regular shapes like rectangles (such as used in a border).

GLASS COSTS (costs will vary by locality and availability)

Antique Glass—may run from $2.50 to $9.00 a square foot (gold streakies)
Cathedral Glass—from $1.70 to $3.00 a square foot
Opalescent Glass—from $2.50 to $3.50 a square foot
Blenko Glass—from $3.00 to $4.50 a square foot

Remember that stained glass is not like paint. If you run out of a particular color, you may not be able to find that exact colored glass when you next return to the studio or craft store.

Section 6
Glass Cutting

Learning the skill of glass cutting probably creates the most anxiety among beginners. In truth, it is not a complicated skill, but, of the basic stained glass techniques, it is the one which requires the most practice.

RECOMMENDED TOOLS AND MATERIALS

GLASS CUTTER:
A stylus with a sharpened steel wheel used to score the glass. Fletcher 02 or Red Devil 023 is recommended for most glass. Fletcher 07 is recommended for scoring opalescent glass.

LUBRICANT:
A mixture of equal parts of 3 in One oil and kerosene is used to clean and lubricate the wheel of the cutter.

PLATE PLIERS:
Used for pulling (breaking) away the glass along the score line. The 6″ plate pliers with ½″ jaw width is recommended. Ordinary household pliers may be substituted.

GROZZING PLIERS:
Used to chew or chip unwanted bits from glass edge. Recommended are grozzing pliers with ¼″ jaws. The serrations in the glass cutter may be used as a substitute.

CUTTING SURFACE:
A soft-backed material on which the sheet of glass is placed. Recommended are each of the following alternatives: a soft wood board such as ¾″ plywood (18″ × 24″) covered with 2 or 3 layers of felt; a sample square of tightly woven rug; Upsom board (pressed paper); plywood covered with a piece of rubber hall runner.

SAFETY GOGGLES:
If you don't wear eye glasses, wear a pair of inexpensive plastic safety glasses when cutting glass.

BENCH BRUSH:
Used to clear your work board of small glass bits. An old floor scrubbing brush works very well.

SILICON CARBIDE STONE:
A flat hand held sharpening stone used to grind smooth the rough edges of shaped glass pieces.

HOLDING THE CUTTER
1. Hold the cutter as shown in Figure 1.
2. Keep your wrist firmly locked.
3. The angle of your cutter to the glass should be about 60°.
4. Before scoring the glass, lubricate the cutter.

MAKING THE SCORE

1. Begin learning to cut (score) glass by practicing on window pane glass.
2. Stand about 12″ away from the workbench with the glass flat on the bench in front of you.
3. Bend over at the waist with your cutting arm extended straight out in front of you. (On large pieces of glass it is not necessary to hold the glass down on the bench with your other hand.)
4. Place the cutter 1/8″ from the edge of the top of the glass and pull the cutter straight back towards you, exerting about 15 pounds of pressure.
5. Try to apply constant pressure as you make the score.
6. Stop the score 1/8″ before you come to the bottom edge of the glass. Avoid going off the glass with the cutter, as it may chip the glass and dull the cutter.
7. Whenever possible, always cut from the top edge of the glass back towards yourself.

NEVER GO OVER A SCORE LINE TWICE!

SEPARATING THE GLASS

All glass is separated from the larger working glass by applying pressure *underneath* the score line. Remember, always keep the side of the glass on which you've made the score facing up towards you.

1. Large Pieces—When the score line is more than 4″ away from one edge of the glass, break away large pieces by using any of the three methods shown in Figure 2 (straight scores only).

1. Recommended Position for Holding the Glass Cutter

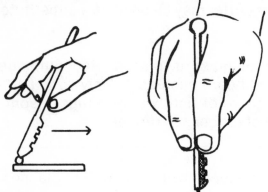

2. Part Medium Sized Straight Line Scores with Thumbs Parallel to Score Line on Each Side

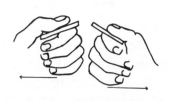

Break down and away with each wrist simultaneously

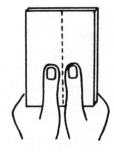

3. Break Off Large Piece By:

(A) Using the Table Edge

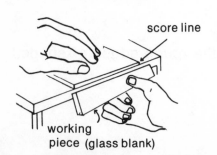

score line

working piece (glass blank)

Hold in place then lift glass slightly and snap down

(B) Cutter Under the Score

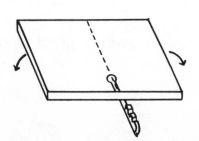

Place one hand on each side of score line and press down

(C) Using a Ruler or Yardstick Score line directly over one edge of ruler

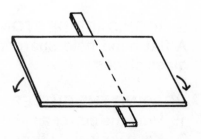

Place one hand on each side of ruler and press down

2. Medium Pieces—When the score line is more than 1″ but less than 4″ away from one edge of the glass, use the method shown in Figure 3 (straight scores only).
3. Small Pieces—When the score line is less than 1″ from the edge of the glass, take the plate or household pliers and place them next to one end of the scored line; pull down and away with one hand holding the glass and the other holding the pliers. (See figures 4 and 5.) You can also use the serrated edge of the glass cutter. (See Figure 6.)
4. Tapping—Long, gently curving scores as well as straight scores can be separated by tapping underneath the score line as shown in Figure 7. The tapping will start a "run," which is indicated by the score line appearing to widen. Once the run starts, advance your tapping ¼″ in front of the run.

4. Recommended Method of Holding Plate and Grozzing Pliers

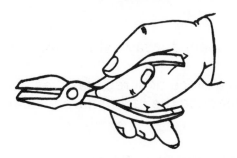

5. Pulling Off Small Straight Line Scores with Pliers

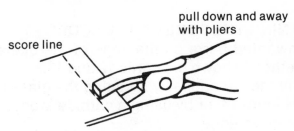

pull down and away with pliers

score line

Nose of pliers is positioned just up to the score line and closer to one edge of glass

6. Use of Cutter Serrations

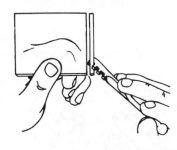

7. Tapping: Hold Glass in one hand as shown, and moderately strike along score line from underneath the glass beginning at one end of the score

5. Curves—Always cut a working piece away from the larger piece of glass first. It saves waste and protects against a random crack running through the large piece. (See Figures 8, 9, and 10.)

8. Cutting Away Concave Glass

Secondary scores

score each and pull away unwanted glass

design piece

After score #1, make score #2 and the secondary scores

(primary score)

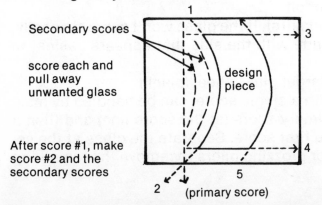

9. Cutting Out a Corner Piece (or semi-circle)

Design piece

(primary score)

Grozz away the small points around the edge of the semi-circle

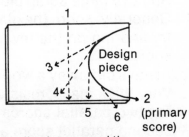

21

6. Scores using the pattern—See Figure 11.

Always leave ½″ excess glass around the primary scores of curved pieces. This greatly aids in getting a good, clean separation of the glass.

10. Cutting a Circular Shape

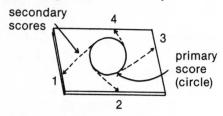

(1) Make primary score first
(2) Make secondary scores to release circle
(3) Pull away glass in the sequence shown

11. Cutting Glass Using a Pattern As a Guide

First score and remove the excess glass

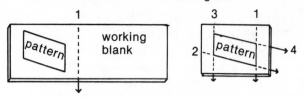

Hold pattern firmly in place with one hand and make the score, guiding cutter wheel along edge of pattern. After each score, pull away the glass.

CLEANING THE EDGE OF THE SCORE

1. Unwanted burrs on the edge of the glass can be cleaned away using either of the methods shown in figures 12 and 13.
2. Dull the cut edges by scraping the glass edge with a piece of scrap glass, as shown in Figure 14, or by using a carbide stone. This will reduce the razor sharpness along the glass edge.

12. Grozzing Unwanted Bits with Pliers

Gently
Avoid Squeezing

14. Dulling the Cut Glass Edges

Run scrap glass (1) along edge of window glass (2) at nearly 90° angle. Repeat on all sides.

13. Grozzing Unwanted Bits with the Cutter

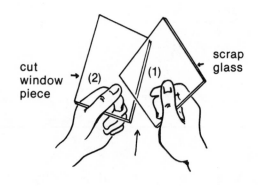

GENERAL GUIDES TO BETTER CUTTING

1. Keep cutter well lubricated.
2. Keep cutting surface brushed clean of glass bits at all times.
3. Remove large scrap pieces from the workbench.
4. Generally, score the glass on the smooth side first. If the glass won't separate easily, try scoring on the reverse side; then continue with the side that appears easiest to score.
5. Always cut away a working piece from the larger glass sheet (blank).
6. Very thick glass, resistant to separation with a single score, can be handled by making two parallel scores. First, make the primary score (at the score line) and then a second parallel score about ½″ next to the first score. Separate the glass at the second score by tapping; then use the plate or grozzing pliers to remove the remaining glass up to the primary score.

7. When cutting opalescent glass, determine which side scores best by using several scrap pieces.
8. Flashed glass usually cuts best by scoring on the thicker (base) side of the glass.
9. Exceptionally hard glass, such as all reds and several of the yellows, may separate better by tapping rather than by pulling away with pliers. Typically, they score best on the reverse side. Experiment on scrap glass first.

PRACTICE! PRACTICE! PRACTICE!
THINK OUT YOUR SEQUENCE OF SCORES BEFORE BEGINNING!

SHAPES TO AVOID
1. Avoid designing interior right angle lines.
2. It's possible to cut a "donut" of glass, but it usually results in great waste and frustration.
3. Long, straight, or curved narrow shapes resulting in a thin narrow point should be cut as several pieces, not as one long piece.

Section 7
Leading

Leading or glazing is the assembly of the cut glass pieces by using channels of lead (called came) to hold the glass in place.

RECOMMENDED TOOLS AND MATERIALS

Tools—caming knife, sharpened 1½" stiff putty knife, reverse sharpened linoleum knife or Franciscan lead cutter; lathekin to open up lead channels; lead vise or boat clamp to hold lead when stretching it; right angle square; hammer.

Materials—Farrier's (horseshoe) nails or 1½" hard nails to hold the glass in place; 1" × 2" pine wood strips to hold the window in place during assembly (enough to completely frame the window); ¾" plywood sheet at least 6" wider and longer than the window size; lead (came) to hold the glass in place; carbide stone and 3 in One oil to sharpen caming knife.

TYPES OF LEAD CAME

Most lead is available in 6' or 7' lengths and costs between $1 and $2 a came, depending upon the width of the lead leaf (crown). Figure 1 shows the more common types of came available. The term "H" came is used for double channeled lead and "U" came is used for single channeled lead (sometimes used around the perimeter of small panels). One other type of came sometimes used for its greater strength is *zinc* came. It is more difficult to work with and between 50 to 100% more expensive.

1. Round lead is most often used in windows of traditional design.
2. Flat lead is most often used in windows of contemporary design (however, round lead may also be appropriate).
3. Lead widths (3/8", 1/4", 3/16") may vary within the window design, but usually you do not mix round and flat leads within a single panel.
4. It's recommended that 5/8" or 1/2" lead be used around the perimeter of the window.
5. For your first window project, use 1/4" lead, as the more narrow widths require much more accurate cutting and glazing.
6. Lead also is available in two heart heights (height between bottom and top lead leafs). Standard height will readily accommodate up to 3/16" glass. The taller heart height is used for thicker glass, particularly with Blenko glass, which tends to run thicker than antique or cathedral.
7. Keep the lead wrapped in newspaper or an old sheet to retard oxidation, which interferes with soldering.

STRETCHING THE LEAD

All lead should be stretched prior to glazing. Stretch one full came at a time. Place one end of the came in a lead vise or boat clamp (which should be screwed down on one corner of the workbench) and, holding the other end of the came with pliers, pull straight back until the came stretches and firms up. If the came is twisted, straighten it out as you pull. You'll get the feel of the amount of stretching with practice. Don't jerk the came, but apply an even pull. If the lead breaks off at either end, you pulled too hard. (See Figure 2.)

1. Lead (Came)

"H" came (flat)

"H" came (round)

"U" came

face 1/4" (crown)

heart height 3/16"

heart width 1/16"

leaf

2. Stretching Lead

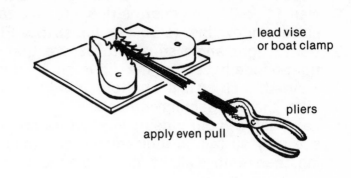

lead vise or boat clamp

pliers

apply even pull

CUTTING THE LEAD

Use any of the recommended types of knives to cut the lead. Keep the knife sharpened, using a carbide honing stone and oil. Sharpen the knife with the blade almost flat on the oiled stone, using a circular motion. Sharpen the knife on both sides.

1. Use either a lead knife or a 1½" to 2" sharpened stiff blade putty knife for cutting lead. (See Figure 3.) Wiggle knife gently as you cut through the face, over the heart of the lead.
2. If you rush the cut, you'll crush the lead. Even with good cutting practice, the leaf of the lead may squash somewhat. Use the lathekin or knife blade to open and flatten the leaf, if necessary. (See Figure 4.)
3. Practice cutting on small pieces of the lead came first. Always place the lead on a hard surface when cutting.
4. Lead is soft so handle it gently.

3. Cutting Lead

Wiggle knife sideways as you apply pressure.

Press slowly but firmly over the heart.

Press Straight Down!

4. Use of Lathekin

crimped channel facing up

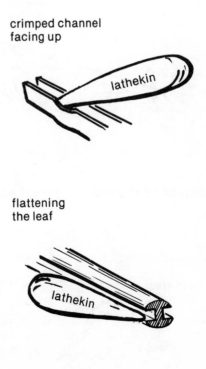

lathekin

flattening the leaf

lathekin

SETTING UP FOR LEADING THE WINDOW

1. Tape the full-sized cutline drawing on a sheet of ¾″ plywood. (See Figure 5.)
2. Nail 1″ × 2″ pine board strips, cut to size, along one length and width of the full-sized window lines (perimeter lines). (See Figure 6.)
3. Use a right angle square to assure that the working corner is at 90°. (If you're right-handed, set up the right angle boards in the bottom left corner; if left-handed, set it up in the bottom right-hand corner.)
4. Miter the intersecting corner lead.
5. Lay each of your glass pieces in its proper position on the drawing and check to see they all fall on their related cut lines. Correct any over-sized pieces by grozzing, then remove all the glass from the drawing.

MEASURING LEAD TO FIT

1. It's too cumbersome to handle the whole 7′ length of lead came, so cut off working strips roughly measured to provide some excess over the amount needed.
2. Shape your working came strip around the glass piece and mark it with the knife.
3. Then place the working strip on the workbench and cut at the mark.
4. When measuring the working came strip, you have to leave room for the overlay of the leaf of the intersecting lead. (See Figure 7.)
5. See figures 8, 9, and 10 for information on proper cut angles on intersecting lead.

5. Setting Up the Board   **6.**

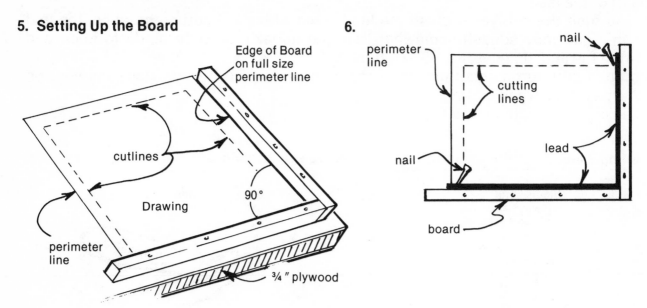

7. Overlap of Leaf of Intersecting Lead

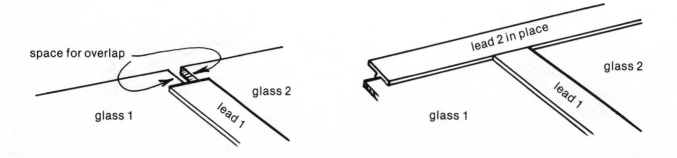

26

8. Proper Angles of Lead Cuts on Intersecting Lead

a. Corner Lead

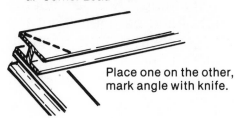

Place one on the other, mark angle with knife.

b. Completed Miter

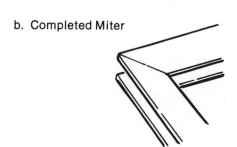

9.

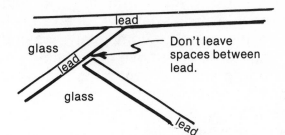

Don't leave spaces between lead.

10. Join Leaded Circle of Glass at an Intersection of Lead

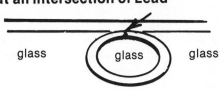

LEADING THE WINDOW

1. Take the first piece of glass and fit it into the left-hand corner of the perimeter lead.
2. Use the blade of the lead knife to raise the glass into the leaf of the came.
3. Tap the glass piece in place, using the back of the lead knife.
4. When the glass is in place, check to see that the unleaded glass edges fall on their cut lines. If the edges extend past, the next piece will not fit properly. Using the grozzing pliers or glass cutter serrations, chew away the glass edges for final fitting.
5. Place a piece of scrap lead on the outside glass edge and tap Farrier's nails in to hold the glass in place. (See figures 11 and 12.)
6. Measure the next piece of lead, cut to size, fit around glass, and secure with nails.
7. Take the next piece of glass; repeat steps 1 through 6. (See figures 13 and 14.)

11.
Place scrap lead against edge of glass, place nail straight up tightly against scrap lead & tap nail into board.

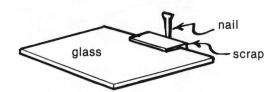

12. Sequence of Leading

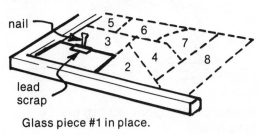

Glass piece #1 in place.

13.

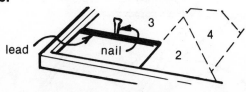

Lead cut short & positioned along top of piece #1.

14.

Piece #3 in place & separated by horizontal lead.

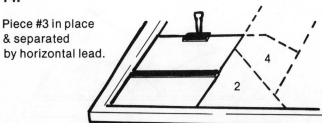

27

8. Think out the sequence in which you must do the leading of the glass pieces so you won't box yourself in and find yourself unable to fit in the next glass piece. You should always have two open ends to work with. (See figures 15 and 16.)

9. When the panel is completely assembled, take the remaining 1″ × 2″ boards and cut to size. Remove the retaining nails from the right-hand perimeter, put the board in place and gently tap it against the window edge; then nail the board in place. Repeat this process for the top perimeter. (See Figure 17.)

10. Check all lead joints (intersections) for spaces. Fill any spaces with slivers of lead to prevent solder form falling through. (See next section.)

11. Check to assure that all four window corners are square.

12. The assembled window is now ready for preparation for soldering.

BARRING

If the glass window panel is much greater than four square feet it is necessary to attach a steel or solid brass bar horizontally across the inside surface of a section approximately every 20″ of the window length. This will prevent the window from sagging.

1. Solder stiff copper wire lengths along each inside lead intersection of the barring line and the perimeter lead. (Figure 18.)

2. Place the steel bar or brass bar (3/16″ wide × 1/8″ thick) (cut to size) on top of the soldered wire lengths.

3. Twist the wire lengths around the bar, solder and cut off the excess wire. (Figure 19.)

Usually the bar is run horizontally along the inside facing of the leaded window.

15.

Lead cut short & in position
along vertical edge of pieces #2 & #4.

16. Lead mitered & in place
along edge of piece #2.

17. When completely leaded, tap boards "A" & "B" in direction of arrows, check for squareness then nail in place.

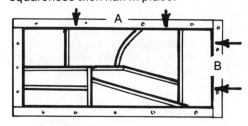

18. Solder stiff copper wire to inside lead joints

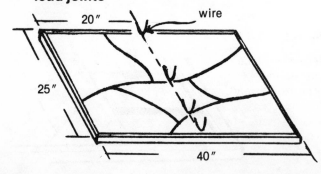

19. Lay in bar, twist wire, solder and trim

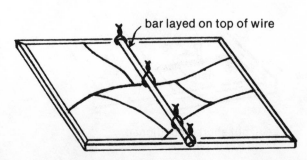

28

Section 8
Soldering

When the entire window is leaded, solder is applied to each intersection or joint of lead to bond the lead strips together.

RECOMMENDED TOOLS AND MATERIALS
(1) solid (no core) solder—1/8″, 60/40 or 50/50 (60% tin/40% lead)
(2) Weller Soldering Iron—80 or 100 watt, 3/8″ chisel tip (SP80, SP100) or Weller Tempmatic—150 watt, ¼″ chisel tip
(3) soldering iron stand (or large metal bottle cap)
(4) oleic acid—flux   (5) flux brush   (6) sponge   (7) wire brush

PREPARATION
1. If the tip of the soldering iron is not tinned (i.e., coated with solder) then you should (1) heat the iron (2) melt a drop of solder onto a can lid on which you have placed a few drops of oleic acid (3) dip the iron tip into the melted solder and acid (4) wipe the tip with a rag.
2. Use a small stiff wire brush to clean the lead at each intersection or joint. This improves the bonding of the solder to the lead. (See Figure 1.)
3. Apply sparingly the flux (oleic acid) to each joint with the flux brush (a small ¼″ hair or flexible wire brush—Figure 2).

SOLDERING
1. Lay about 1/8″ to 1/4″ of solder wire on the joint. (See Figure 3.)
2. Place the flat edge of the heated soldering iron directly on the solder and press down. (See Figure 3.)
3. When the solder melts and flows evenly over the joint, lift iron straight up, away from the joint. (See Figure 4.)

1. Wire Brush the Joints (shaded area)

2. Apply Flux Sparingly at the Joints (shaded area)

3. Lay Solder Wire on Joint and Press Down with Iron Directly over Joint

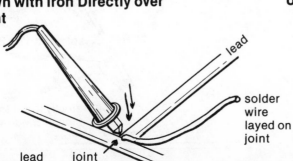

lead   joint

solder wire layed on joint

4. When Solder Melts, Pull Iron Straight Up and Away From Joint

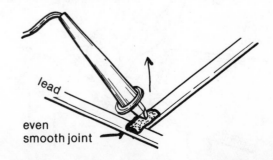

even smooth joint

GUIDES FOR CLEANLY SOLDERED JOINTS

1. Be sure your iron tip is tinned, i.e., coated with solder.
2. Use less solder rather than too much. It is easier to add solder than to remove it.
3. Keep a clean iron tip by periodically passing the hot tip through a dampened slit sponge.
4. Apply the flux (oleic acid) sparingly to the joints.
5. Test the heat of your iron by placing it on a piece of scrap lead. If the lead melts, your iron is too hot.
6. If the solder and flux bubble and blacken, your iron is too hot.
7. If, when you remove the iron from the joint, the solder peaks (like meringue) then your iron is too cold.
8. Do not smear or push the melted solder around the joint as it will result in a rough, ridged joint. Let heat and gravity flow the solder over the joint.
9. If the solder doesn't bond to the lead, the lead was probably dirty and/or not fluxed. In this case, scrape the joint with a wire brush and then apply the flux and resolder the joint.
10. For any joints where the lead strips don't butt tightly together, cut little scraps of lead to fill in the spaces before you solder.

GENERAL WINDOW INSTRUCTIONS

1. Completely solder one side of the window. Check soldering at each joint. (See Figure 5.)
2. Turn window over, using the technique shown in figures 6, 7, and 8.
3. Solder the reverse side of the window.
4. Reinspect all joints for firm soldering and overall good appearance.

5. How to Turn a Window Soldered on One Side

top side is soldered

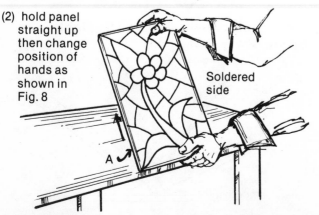

6. Soldered Side Still Faces You

push window to edge then raise Side B

Soldered side

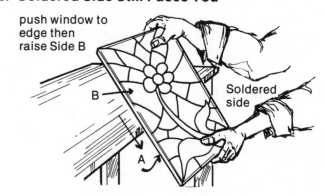

7.

(1) then push window B up on table

(2) hold panel straight up then change position of hands as shown in Fig. 8

Soldered side

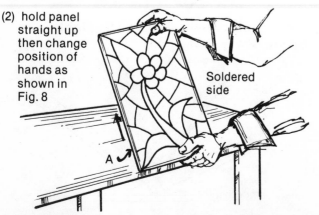

8.

(1) first push edge B towards back of table while supporting unsoldered side

unsoldered side A → ← soldered side B

(2) slowly lower the soldered side of window onto the table

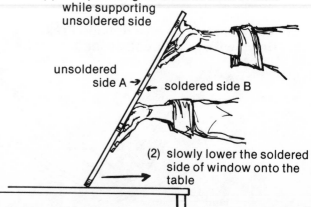

Section 9
Cementing

Cementing is the application of a caulking compound to the soldered window in order to make it waterproof and to tighten the glass within the lead channels.

RECOMMENDED CEMENT MIXTURES

Recommended by Mollica Studio
4 parts Whiting
2 parts Plaster of Paris
1½ parts Turpentine
1 part Boiled Linseed Oil
1 part Portland Cement
Sprinkle powdered Lampblack to color

Recommended by Luciano Studio
1 pound DAP Glazing Compound 1012
1 cup Turpentine
2 handfuls Whiting
Lampblack to Color
Mix to a thick mud consistency. Add Whiting to thicken; add Turpentine to thin.

RECOMMENDED TOOLS AND MATERIALS
(1) a 2-gallon container
(2) two flat scrub (or bench) brushes with stiff bristles (1″)
(3) sharpened pencil-sized stick (such as a manicure "orange" stick)
(4) 1″ stiff putty knife or flat lathekin
(5) sawdust (optional)

CEMENTING
1. This is a messy task so old clothes should be worn when cementing.
2. Lay newspapers over a cleaned work area and lay the window on top of the papers.
3. Take one scrub brush and dip it into the cement mixture; then transfer the cement to the window.
4. Using a circular motion, rub and push the cement over the glass and under all the lead leaf. The object is to force the cement between the leaf and the glass. (See Figure 1.)
5. Continue to add cement over this side of the window until no vacant areas remain between the lead and the glass.
6. Lightly press down the lead leaf with the putty knife or lathekin (optional).
7. Sprinkle several handfuls of Whiting (or sawdust) over the window surface; spread the Whiting with a rag.
8. Remove the excess cement with the brush you've been using.
9. Sprinkle on more Whiting (or sawdust) and brush dry with the second (clean) scrub brush.
10. Let this side of the window lie flat and dry for 2 to 3 hours.
11. Turn over the window and repeat steps 3 through 10 for this side of the window.
12. Take the sharpened stick and remove all excess cement from the edges of the lead and from the joints, where it tends to collect. Follow this procedure for both sides of the window. (See Figure 2.)
13. Sprinkle Whiting (or sawdust) on the window and polish with the clean brush. Repeat on the reverse side of the window.
14. Let the window lie flat for 36 hours before applying any final treatment and installation—sections 10 and 11.

1. Push Cement Between Glass & Lead Leaf

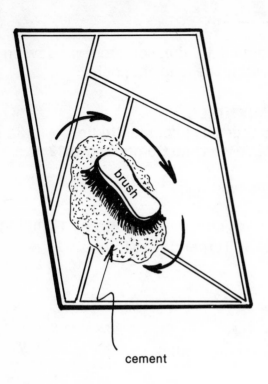

cement

2. Remove Excess Dried Cement with a Sharp Stick

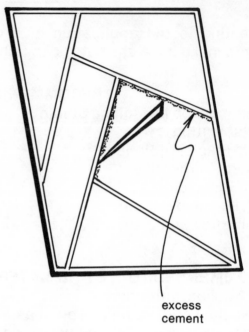

excess cement

Do not get the point of the stick under the lead

Section 10
Final Treatment and Window Cleanup

For an added effect, the lead and solder in your completed window can receive one of the final treatments listed below.

PREPARING THE WINDOW
1. Use a manicure "orange" stick or similarly sharpened wood stick to remove any cement protruding from the lead came.
2. Clean all glass, lead, and solder thoroughly, using Whiting (or sawdust) and a scrub brush.
3. Wipe the window clean with a damp sponge.

DARKENING THE LEAD AND SOLDER
Each of the following three alternatives is effective for darkening or prematurely aging the lead and solder in your window.

Alternative 1—Studio Prepared Solution
1. Dissolve 3 fluid ounces of Allen's Brand Tinners Acid with 2 tablespoons of Copper Sulfate Powder.
2. Using an artist brush (or toothbrush) apply the above solution to the lead and solder. Let it stand for 2 to 3 minutes.
3. Wipe the treated area gently with a soft cloth.
4. Reapply solution to increase and unify the darkening effect.
5. Wipe excess solution from glass.

Clean sawdust rubbed over a leaded window, using a clean scrub brush, cleans and polishes the glass to a high luster. However, the abrasiveness of the sawdust will remove most of the "final treatment" from the lead.

Alternative 2—Black Patina (from Nervo Studios, Berkeley, Ca.)
1. Lead and solder must be clean and dry.
2. Follow Step 2 in Alternative 1 above, using the Black Patina.
3. Wash the window thoroughly with water (including the glass).
4. Repeat the above procedure for a darker patina.
5. Black Patina also works well on foiled windows.

Alternative 3—Gun Blue (from hardware or sporting goods store)
1. Use a small artist paint brush (or toothbrush) and apply the Gun Blue to the soldered joints only. Avoid getting the Gun Blue on the glass. Let stand for 2 to 3 minutes.
2. Wash the window thoroughly, as Gun Blue will stain the glass if it is allowed to stand.

Antique Patina for Foiled Windows
1. Dissolve in 1 cup of heated water 1 tablespoon Copper Sulfate Powder and 2 to 3 drops of Hydrochloric Acid.
2. Follow steps 2 through 5 in Alternative 1.
3. With each additional application of solution, the solder will take on a deepening brownish-copper effect.
4. The treated solder can be buffed with a soft dry cloth or 000 steel wool for a polished effect.

WINDOW CLEANUP

Commercial brand Glass Wax is the easiest and most effective agent for cleaning and polishing the glass without removing the treated effect on the lead and solder.

An alternative to Glass Wax is a commercial spray preparation sold by Franciscan Glass company, Palo Alto, Calif.

After you have invested all the energy and hours to make the window, take the care and the time to do a thorough cleanup job on the window.

Section 11
Window Installation

This section discusses the techniques for installing a window (1) in a wood or metal sash (2) over an existing window (3) by hanging it within a larger window.

RECOMMENDED TOOLS & MATERIALS
Tools—hammer, 1″ wide blade putty knife, screwdriver, silicone sealant
Wood Sash—glazing points, or 1″ brads, wood putty, wood stops
Metal Sash—metal sash clips, metal sash putty.

Compare the measurements of your stained glass window to that of the existing window before removing the existing glass from the window sash.

INSTALLATION IN WOOD SASH (See Figure 1.)
1. Remove the old putty facing with a putty knife (or chisel) and remove the old glass.
2. If the window is held in with exterior wood stops, remove the stops from the window and then remove the old glass.
3. Use the putty knife to clean any remaining putty from sash.
4. Place your leaded window into the window opening for another size check. If it fits too tightly, trim away the edges of the perimeter lead with the came knife. If the fit is too loose, you can tighten it up and square it off by using wood "shims" (shaved pieces of wood) after the inside sash facing has been puttied. Now remove the leaded window from the opening.
5. Take a handful of wood sash putty and soften the putty by kneading it with your hands.
6. Place half of the putty in one hand and run a bead of putty against the vertical face of the inside stop by using the heel of your hand to place and press the putty against the stop. Then clean your hands.
7. Place the leaded window in the opening and square it off, using shims if necessary.
8. Drive 2 glazing points or brads into the sash along each of the 4 sides of the window.
9. Using another handful of softened putty, run another bead of putty where the leaded section of the window meets the wood.
10. It is recommended that you place wood stops along the window on the exterior side as well. Measure the stops to fit snugly within the sash and secure them with brads.
11. Clean the excess putty from both sides of the window and clean the glass.

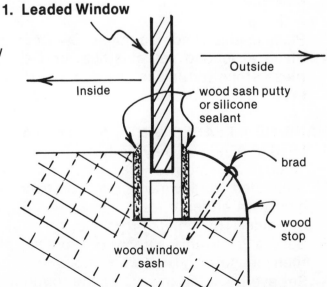

1. Leaded Window

Outside

Inside

wood sash putty or silicone sealant

brad

wood stop

wood window sash

INSTALLATION IN METAL SASH
(See Figure 2.)

1. Remove existing stops (if any) by unscrewing them. If no screws are visible, the metal stops are probably the snap-on type which can be pried loose.
2. Metal sash windows without stops are held in place with metal spring clips, which can be removed using a screwdriver as you remove the old putty.
3. Follow steps 4 through 7 preceding.
4. Replace the metal spring clips in their respective holes, making certain that they press against the perimeter of your leaded window.
5. Run another bead of putty around the leaded section, using the putty knife to smooth and clean away excess putty.
6. If the metal window sash used stops, reset these stops after running the bead of putty; then clean away the excess putty.

2. Leaded Window

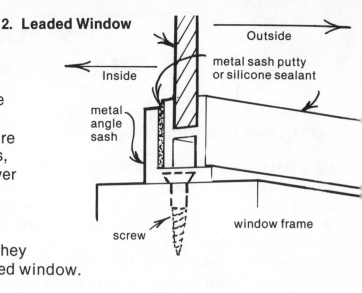

3. Inside Sash

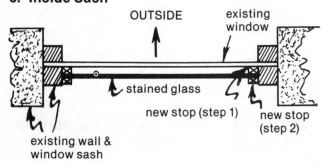

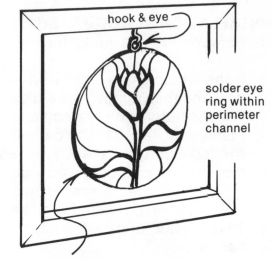

4.

Fill perimeter "H" channel with solder to prevent sagging.

INSTALLATION OVER AN EXISTING WINDOW (See Figure 3.)

1. If the leaded window is not to be permanently installed, you can set it inside the existing window.
2. Measure stops to fit snugly around the inside window sash and secure the stops with brads.
3. Place leaded window against new stops and square off with shims, if necessary.
4. Place a second set of stops around the perimeter of your window and secure these stops to the sash with brads. No putty or silicone sealer is necessary as the existing "outside window" is sealed and waterproofed.

HANGING A LEADED WINDOW WITHIN A LARGER EXISTING WINDOW

1. Leaded windows may be hung inside, in front of a larger existing window. Round "medallion windows" are particularly pleasing when hung this way. (See Figure 4.)
2. As leaded windows will sag and stretch with time, you must frame the leaded window with either 1″ × 2″ or 2″ × 2″ wood strips with a ½″ × ¾″ inset cut on one side. (This procedure is used for square or rectangular windows.)
3. Secure the frame with wood screws, place the leaded window within the inset, then measure and nail wood stops to hold the window within the frame.
4. Set eye hooks in the top of the frame and suspend the window by a light chain or macraméd cords from the top inside sash.

Section 12
Copper Foil Technique

This section describes the copper foil process for window assembly as an alternative to the leaded window process.

The copper foil process is often used when a window design is comprised of many small pieces of glass. In such a case the leaded technique would be unwieldy and/or would result in a bulky appearance. The copper foil process is also used in place of the leaded technique when greater strength is required because the window size, if leaded, would require barring (which may be undesirable from a design viewpoint). Foiled windows are not subject to stretching and sagging as are leaded windows. Further, the solder beads formed in the foiled process can be textured for added design effect.

RECOMMENDED TOOLS AND MATERIALS
Glass Cutting—same as listed in Section 6
Foil—adhesive-backed copper foil (3/16″, 1/4″, 3/8″, 1/2″ widths)
Exacto Knife
Fid or Lathekin
Soldering—same as listed in Section 8
All Purpose Flux
Cementing—not required
Final Treatment—See Section 10.

CUT LINES FOR COPPER FOIL
Refer to figures 1 and 2 prior to making your cutline drawing and cutting your patterns for a foiled window. As shown in the figures, you do not provide a 1/16″ space for the lead heart when making a cutline pattern for a foiled window.

1. Cutlines for Leaded Glass

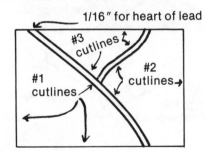

2. Cutlines for Foiled Glass

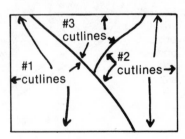

FOILING THE GLASS
1. Use adhesive-backed copper foil. Foil is available in 36 yard rolls of 3/16″, 1/4″, 3/8″, and 1/2″ widths.
2. For most glass, 3/16″ or 1/4″ width foil is sufficient.
3. Before wrapping the edges of your cut glass pieces with the adhesive-backed foil, wash all the glass to remove dirt and oil. This will improve the sticking of the foil to the glass edges.
4. Smooth any rough and jagged edges of the cut glass pieces with a silicone carbide stone.

5. Work your foil in strips that are long enough to go completely around the glass and overlap the starting end by at least ¼".
6. Run the foil along the edge of the glass with an even amount of overhang on either side of the glass. (See figures 3 and 4.)
7. Press the foil to the glass edge with a lathekin, fid, or flat piece of wood. (See Section 13.)
8. Now press the foil that extends past the edges of the glass down on each side of the glass.
9. Lay the glass piece down flat and run the fid firmly over the foil to fix it to the glass. Turn the glass over and press the foil down with the fid. (See Figure 5.)
10. Check to verify that the overlap on each side of the glass is even in width. If not, use an Exacto knife on the large width and remove the excess foil. Then lay that piece aside and foil the next piece.

ASSEMBLY OF THE FOILED GLASS PIECES
1. Assembly for foiled glass is similar to that described in Section 7.
2. Nail 1" × 2" wood strips along 2 sides of the perimeter of your cutline drawing, forming a right angle guide (except for circular windows).
3. Place your foiled pieces on the drawing, beginning at the right angle corner, and push them tightly together. Use horseshoe nails to keep the pieces locked in place.
4. When all your pieces are in place within the perimeter of the drawing, nail 2 additional boards along the remaining 2 sides of the window to hold the assembled window firmly in place. Using a right angle guide, check that each corner is at a true 90°.

SOLDERING COPPER FOILED GLASS PIECES
1. Initially, only tack solder the pieces to be joined. To tack solder, place just enough solder to hold the two pieces together on the fluxed area to be joined. (See Figure 6.)

3. Starting the Foil

Be certain that glass is centered over foil so that an even overlap results when the foil is pressed to the sides of the glass.

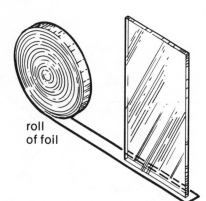

roll of foil

4. Completely Foiled Glass Piece

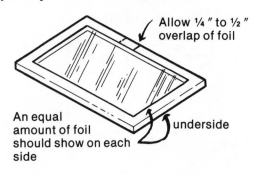

Allow ¼" to ½" overlap of foil

An equal amount of foil should show on each side

underside

5.

Run fid over foiled glass piece on both sides and along the edge as well

6. Foiled Pieces Tack Soldered

wrapped foil

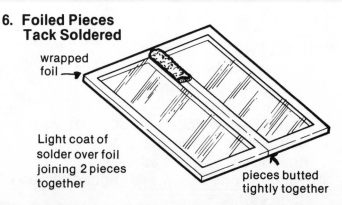

Light coat of solder over foil joining 2 pieces together

pieces butted tightly together

2. When you do your final soldering, you want to completely cover all exposed foil with a bead of solder. To get a good bead, place the solder wire along the length of the pieces to be joined and place your iron tip over the solder. As the solder melts, raise your iron and pull it over the unmelted solder wire until the whole surface has a smooth raised bead of solder. (See figures 7 and 8.)
3. When you have placed an even bead of solder on all the foiled surfaces on one side of the window, turn the window over (using the technique shown in Section 8) and solder the reverse side of the window.
4. The bead of solder can be texturized by randomly placing the heated iron into the bead and then quickly removing it. This results in a finish that is rough rather than smooth.
5. Foiled windows do not require cementing.
6. See Section 10 for final treatment techniques.

There is no rule as to when a foiled window is preferable to a leaded window. The choice is typically made on the basis of design judgements. The copper foiling technique is a more exacting and time consuming process than the leaded technique, but the results can be stunning.

7. Running a Bead of Solder

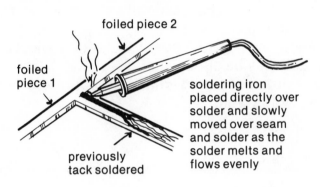

foiled piece 2

foiled piece 1

previously tack soldered

soldering iron placed directly over solder and slowly moved over seam and solder as the solder melts and flows evenly

8. Bead of Solder

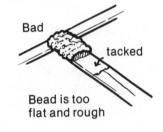

Bad

tacked

Bead is too flat and rough

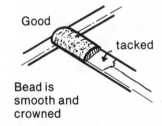

Good

tacked

Bead is smooth and crowned

Section 13
Stained Glass Tools

GLASS CUTTING
1. Glass Cutter—used to score (scratch) the surface of the glass. The Fletcher 02, 2QT, or Red Devil 23 is recommended for most glass. Fletcher 07 is recommended for scoring opalescent glass.
2. Plate Pliers—used for pulling (breaking) away the glass along the score line. Ordinary household pliers may be substituted.
3. Grozzier Pliers—used to chew or chip unwanted bits from the glass edge. The three serrations of the glass cutter are also useful for grozzing.

LEADING
4. Caming Knife—used to cut lead came. The curved edge aids in cutting through the lead, using a rocking motion.
5. Putty Knife—a substitute for the caming knife. Use a stiff 1½" to 2" putty knife sharpened on both sides (shaded area).
6. Lathekin—a tool made of bone, hardwood, or compressed wood and used to manipulate lead came.
7. Tacking Hammer—used to tap in the horseshoe (or Farrier) nails which are used to secure the glass and lead when leading a panel.
8. Horseshoe (or Farrier) Nails—used to keep the lead in position around the cut glass pieces prior to soldering. (1" lathe nails may be substituted.)
9. Lead Vise—used to hold one end of came (lead) securely while you pull the other end to stretch the lead. A boat-jam cleat (9) works well.

FOILING
10. Exacto Knife—used to evenly trim the edges of foiled glass. It is also useful for pattern cutting.
11. Fid—a conical, smooth hardwood spike used to press the foil around the edges of the glass pieces.

SOLDERING
12. Soldering Iron—an 80 to 100 watt iron with a 3/8" chisel tip is suitable for most jobs.
13. Flux Brush—brush used to apply flux to the lead joints and copper foil. (A soft wire brush works well.)
14. Sponge Cleaner—a dampened slit sponge is used to clean the heated soldering iron tip.

	TOOL	TYPE OR BRAND
	cutter	Fletcher 02 general purpose
RECOMMENDED		Fletcher 07 for Opalescent glass
TOOLS FOR	pliers	household for use as grozzing pliers
THE BEGINNER	plate pliers	6" length with ½" jaw width
	soldering iron	Weller 80 watt, 3/8" chisel tip
	lathekin	pressed board
	lead vise	boat-jam cleat
	lead knife	sharpened stiff blade, 2" width putty knife
	hammer	household

Once you have tried the craft and have determined that you are going to seriously continue working in stained glass, the following additional tools are recommended.

TOOL	TYPE OR BRAND
plate pliers	8″ length with 1″ jaw width
grozzing pliers	6″ length with ¼″ jaw width
caming knife	8″ length, leaded handle
soldering iron	Weller W100 with reastat heat control

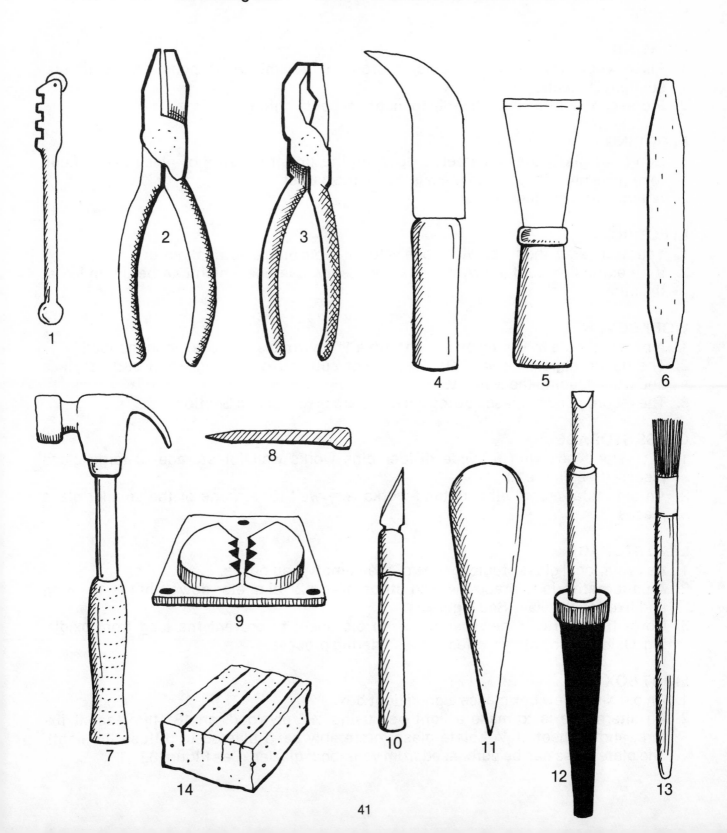

Section 14
Stained Glass Work Area

This section provides guidance in assembling the work area within a limited amount of space. Although a typical stained glass studio layout is the ideal condition, stained glass windows can be assembled at home using a work area no larger than 6′ × 6′.

LIGHTING
1. Place your workbench or table in front of a window, if possible, as natural sunlight is ideal.
2. Florescent lighting is preferable to incandescent lighting.

FLOORING
1. Don't cut glass over a carpeted floor, as the tiny fragments of glass are difficult to remove once they imbed themselves in the carpet.
2. A hard surfaced floor is best.

ELECTRICAL
1. Your work area should provide access to a double plug electrical outlet.
2. If an extension cord (heavy-duty) is necessary, use one which can be grounded at the outlet.

WORKBENCH
1. A bench 3′ wide by 6′ long by 3′ high with a 1″ plywood surface is recommended.
2. The bench should be very stable and not subject to shifting when cutting glass and when leading the window.
3. The recommended glass cutting surfaces are discussed in Section 6.

GLASS STORAGE
1. A plywood box with 6″ wide divider bins works well for storage of large glass pieces. (See Figure 1.)
2. An old metal record album stand works very well for storage of the smaller glass pieces.

LEAD STORAGE
1. Ask your local glass studio for one of their empty lead boxes.
2. An alternative is to drape the lead strips over a 2″ diameter dowel that is 18″ long and fixed to the wall. (See Figure 2.)
3. Cover the lead with newspapers or an old sheet to prevent the lead from oxidizing. Oxidation adversely affects the soldering process.

LIGHT BOX
1. An old X-ray view box makes a good light box.
2. An alternative is to make a light box using ½″ plywood, an 18″ fluorescent fixture, and a sheet of ¼″ plate glass (preferably sand blasted to diffuse the light). The plate glass can be purchased from your local glazier. (See Figure 3.)

1. Glass Storage Box

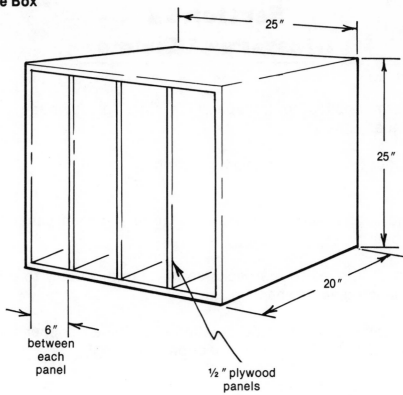

25"

25"

20"

6"
between
each
panel

½" plywood
panels

2. Lead Storage Bar

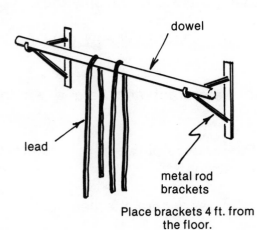

dowel

lead

metal rod
brackets

Place brackets 4 ft. from
the floor.

3. Light Box

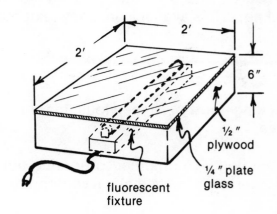

2'

2'

6"

½"
plywood

¼" plate
glass

fluorescent
fixture

Section 15
Glossary of Terms

Antique Glass Term applied to transparent stained glass made by the ancient hand-blown technique.

Antique Patina Copper effect achieved by treating solder with a copper sulfate solution.

Banding Soldering copper wires to the back side of a leaded panel to support and hold the stiffening bar.

Bar Steel stiffener(s) applied to the backside of a large window to prevent the lead from stretching or sagging out of shape.

Bead of Solder A thick coat of solder applied over joined copper foil glass edges and over seams formed by the joined glass sections (beading).

Blenko Antique American hand-blown glass made by the Blenko Glass Company.

Came (lead) Strips of lead milled to standard shapes and sizes and used to hold pieces of stained glass together.

Cathedral Glass Term applied to machine-made stained glass of very even thickness. It is available in many textures and varying degrees of transparency.

Cutline Drawing Used in this book to mean the full-sized window drawing which shows the cut line for each piece of glass within the design.

Caulking (putty) Impervious material used to waterproof and hold a window in place.

Cementing The method of forcing putty into the grooves between the lead leaf and the inserted glass to make it waterproof and to add strength.

Daylight Line The line around each section of glass where the perimeter of lead ends and the glass begins.

Flashed Glass Antique glass with a thin layer of a primary colored glass fused onto the thicker base colored glass (usually white).

Flux Chemical applied to the leaded joints and the copper foiled edges to prevent oxidation during soldering.

Foiling The method of wrapping the edges of cut glass pieces with adhesive-backed copper foil tape.

Foiling Technique Term used in this book for the method of joining cut pieces of glass together using copper foil and solder.

Glass Blank A large piece of glass (also called a working piece of glass) from which smaller pieces of glass will be cut, using a pattern.

Grozz To chew or break away small amounts from a cut glass piece with pliers or the serrations of the glass cutter.

Leading The method of joining cut pieces of glass together by placing strips of lead came between them and applying solder to the lead joints.

Lead Joints The intersection of two or more pieces of lead used in the assembly of cut pieces of glass.

Opalescent Glass Term applied to machine-made glass which is semi-opaque and is used extensively in windows and lampshades. (Also referred to as Opal.)

Oleic Acid Recommended flux to be used in preparing the lead joints to receive the solder.

Patterns Templates used to guide the cutter in scoring a piece of glass to the exact shape desired.

Score Term that refers to scratching the surface of the glass with a glass cutter.

Solder Combination of tin and lead in 1/8″ wide wire (solid core) in one pound rolls. (Term is also used as a verb in this book.)

Stained glass Glass composed of silica sand, iron, soda ash, limestone, borax, plus various metallic oxides for coloring.

Tack Solder To place a small amount of solder on the lead joints or on the edges of foiled glass in order to hold them in place prior to placing a full application of solder.

Tinning To coat the copper tip of the soldering iron with solder. Also used in this book to mean the application of a very thin coat of solder to the lead or foil.

Whiting Powdered calcium carbonate (chalk) used to clean the residue of flux and grime from the soldered glass sections.

Section 16
Available Window Patterns

Section 17
Designs of Old

Anonymous

48

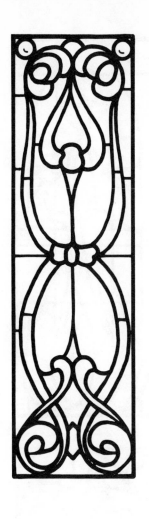

Anonymous

49

Anonymous

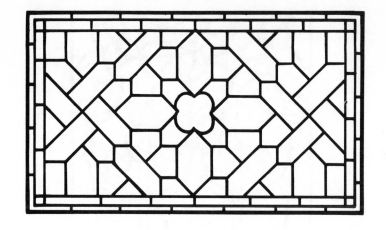

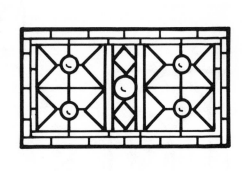

Anonymous

Joanne Nervo   Nervo Art Stained Glass Works   Berkeley, Ca.

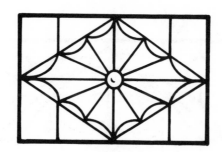

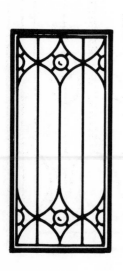

Joanne Nervo   Nervo Art Stained Glass Works   Berkeley, Ca.

54

Joanne Nervo   Nervo Art Stained Glass Works   Berkeley, Ca.

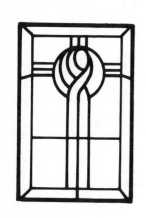

Joanne Nervo   Nervo Art Stained Glass Works   Berkeley, Ca.

John Hogan   Hogan Stained Glass   Los Gatos, Ca.

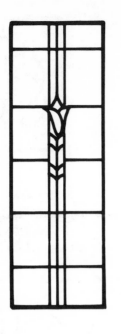

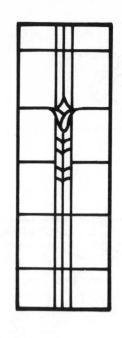

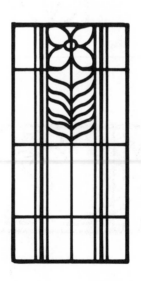

John Hogan   Hogan Stained Glass   Los Gatos, Ca.

Design Staff   Willet Stained Glass Studios   Philadelphia, Pa.

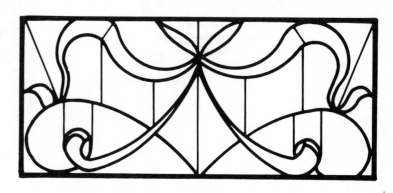

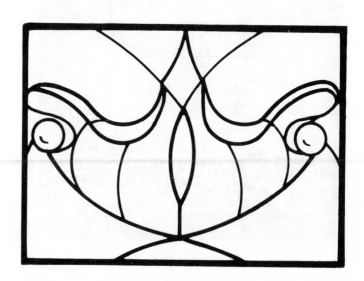

George Schattle   Luciano Stained Glass Art   Palo Alto, Ca.

George Schattle   Luciano Stained Glass Art   Palo Alto, Ca.

Section 18
Contemporary Window Art

Meadow Wind

Raymond Bachtle   Bachtle Studios   Tujunga/Santa Barbara, Ca.

63

Thomas Finsterwald   Finsterwald Art Glass   Santa Cruz, Ca.

Suzanne Blessing   Olszewski Stained Glass   Corpus Christi, Tex.

Frank Drehobl Jr.   Drehobl Bros.   Chicago, Ill.

66

Betty Jane Chang   Chang Stained Glass   Sunnyvale, Ca.

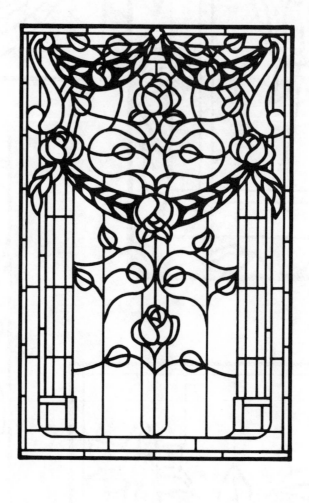

Design Staff   Willett Stained Glass Studios   Philadelphia, Pa.

68

San Francisco Stained Glass   San Francisco, Ca.

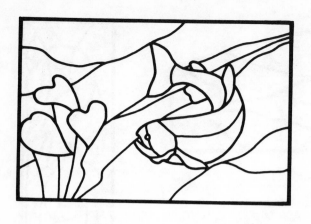

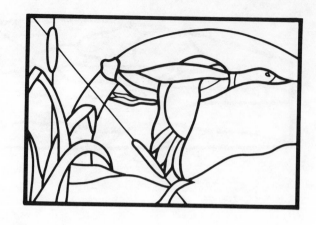

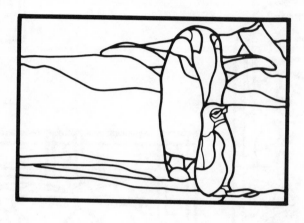

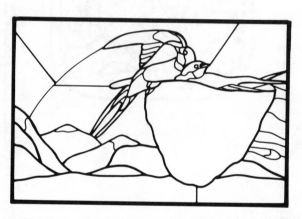

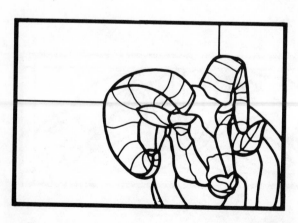

Carol Cullenbine   Cullenbine Stained Glass   Palo Alto, Ca.

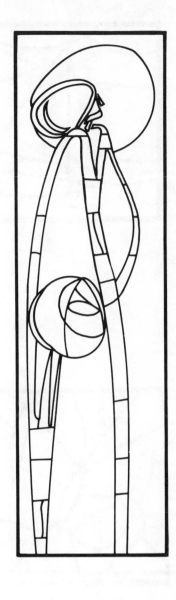

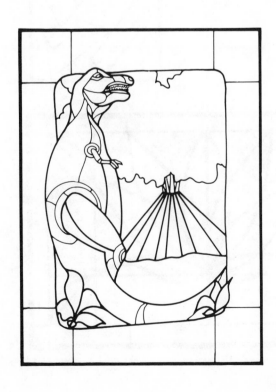

Tim Lantz   Middle Earth Stained Glass   Morgan Hill, Ca.

71

Nancy Broadwell and Adamm Grittlefeld   Adamms Stained Glass Designs   Los Angeles, Ca.

72

Emery and Carol Ann Bernier   Bernier Studio   Wentworth, N.H.

1

2

3

4

5

6

Deirde K. Levine (#1, #3, #6)   Andy Crafts Studio   Wash. D.C.

Ted and Jean Tracy (#2, #4, #5)   Tracey's Stained Glass   Morristown, N.J.

Kristi Carlson   Hidden House of Crafts   Palo Alto, Ca.

Diane Grande   The Studio   Arlington, Va.

Joy   Hidden House of Crafts   Palo Alto, Ca.

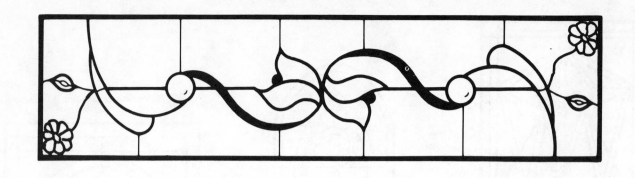

Luciano   Luciano Stained Glass Art   Palo Alto, Ca.

78

Luciano   Luciano Stained Glass Art   Palo Alto, Ca.

Robert W. Hill   Hill/Brusey Stained Glass Studio   Soquel, Ca.

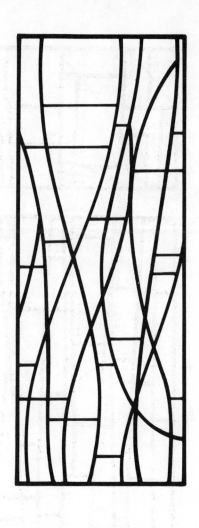

Robert W. Hill   Hill/Brusey Stained Glass Studio   Soquel, Ca.

George Schattle   Luciano Stained Glass Art   Palo Alto, Ca.

Section 19
Project Windows

This section contains the bill of materials for the six windows shown on the front and back covers of the book. The full-size cutline drawings for two of the more difficult windows are contained in the fold-out sheet at the end of the book. The project windows are listed in order of increasing technical difficulty.

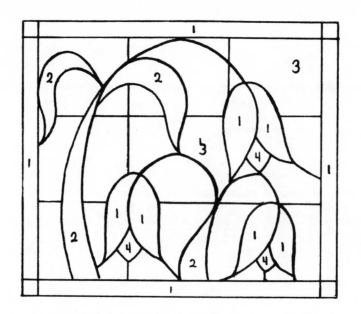

Project:	**SLEEPING TULIPS**		
Designer:	**Roger Bibo**		
Studio:	**Franciscan Glass, Mt. View, California**		
Dimensions:	**21″ × 18″**		

Section	Color	Type	Amount
1	Red/Orange/White	Opalescent	⅔ sq. ft.
2	Green	Opalescent	⅔ sq. ft.
3	Clear	Antique Seedy	2½ sq. ft.
4	Red or Ruby	Antique Clear	16 sq. in.
Lead:	perimeter	½″ round	7 ft
	inside	¼″ round	21 feet
Solder:		50/50	¼ pound

Figures for material amounts include a 25% waste factor. To draw a full-size cutline drawing of the project window use the method described in Section 3.

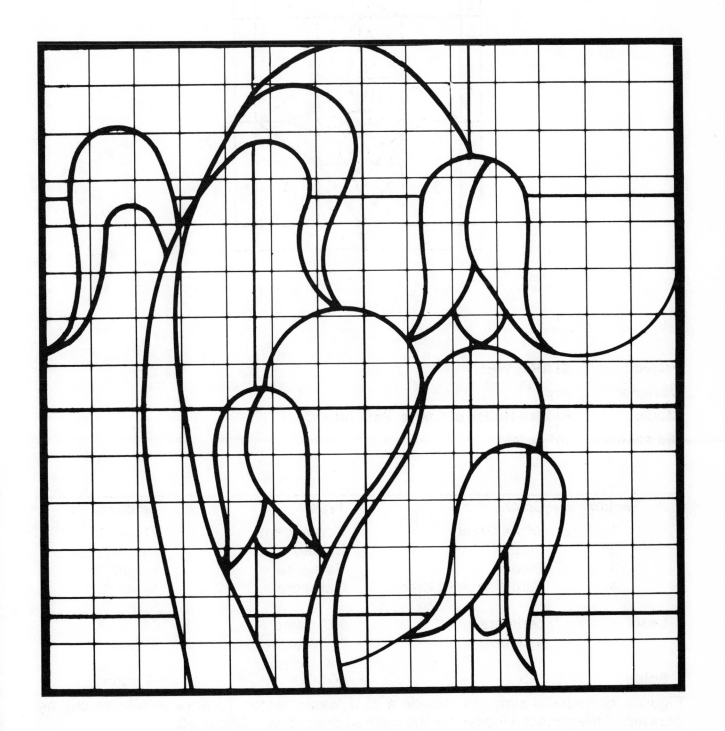

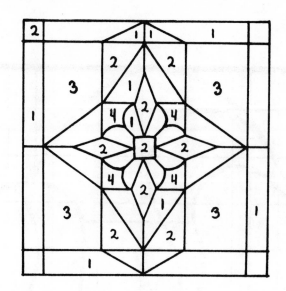

Project: **STARJEWEL**

Designer: **Joy**

Studio: **Hidden House of Crafts, Palo Alto, Ca.**

Dimensions: **20″ × 20″**

Section	Color	Type	Amount
1	White/Green	Opalescent	1¼ sq. ft.
2	Purple	Blenko	1 sq. ft.
3	Purple	Cathedral	1½ sq. ft.
4	Purple or Light Green	Cathedral	¼ sq. ft.
Lead:	perimeter	½″ round	7 ft
	inside	¼″ round	21 feet
Solder:		50/50	¼ pound

Figures for material amounts include a 25% waste factor. To draw a full-size cutline drawing of the project window use the method described in Section 3.

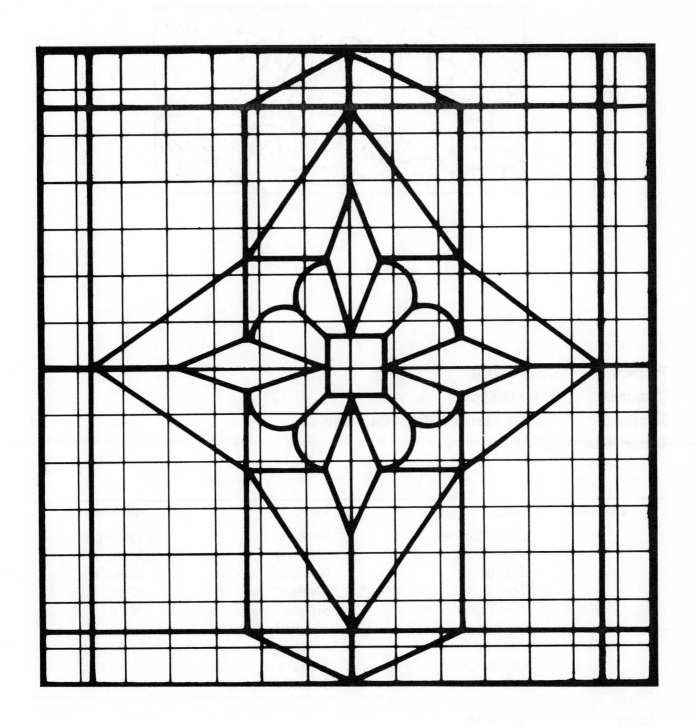

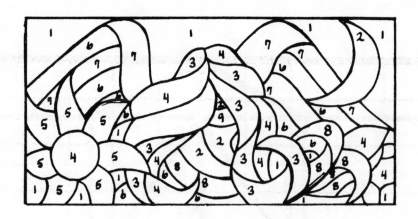

Project: **CELESTRAL**

Designer: **Peter Mollica**

Studio: **Mollica Stained Glass, Berkeley, Ca.**

Dimensions: **29″ × 14″**

Section	Color	Type	Amount
1	Light Purple	Blenko	1 ¼ sq. ft.
2	Blue	Streaky	¼ sq. ft.
3	Orange	Antique	½ sq. ft.
4	Gold	Blenko	¾ sq. ft.
5	Blue/Gold	Streaky	¾ sq. ft.
6	Turquoise	Seedy Antique	½ sq. ft.
7	Deep Blue	Antique	½ sq. ft.
8	Amber/Gold	Streaky	¼ sq. ft.
9	Pink	Streaky	scrap
Lead:	perimeter	½ ″ round	8 ft
	inside	¼ ″ round	28 feet
Solder:		50/50	⅓ pound

Figures for material amounts include a 50% waste factor for glass and a 20% waste factor for lead. To draw a full-size cutline drawing of the project window use the method described in Section 3.

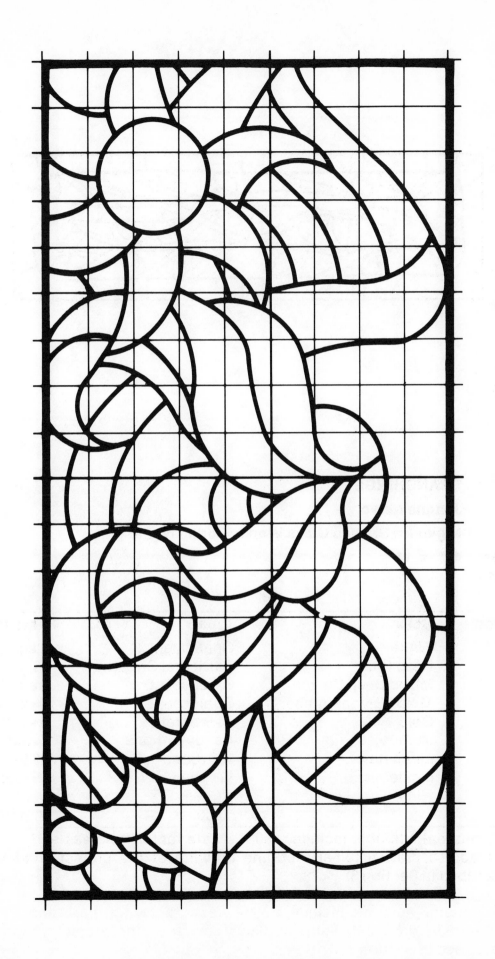

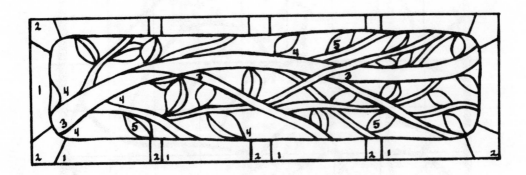

Project: BRANCHINGS

Designer: Joanne Nervo

Studio: Nervo Art Stained Glass Works, Berkeley, Ca.

Dimensions: 46" × 14"

Section	Color	Type	Amount
1	White	Opalescent	2 sq. ft.
2	Deep Blue	Cathedral Streaky	⅓ sq. ft.
3	Mixed Deep Brown	Opalescent	1 sq. ft.
4	Mixed Greens/Amber	Opalescent	⅔ sq. ft.
5	Gold	Cathedral	3 sq. ft.
Lead:	perimeter	½" round	12 feet
	inside	¼" round	35 feet
Solder:		50/50	⅓ pound

Figures for material amounts include a 50% waste factor for glass and a 20% waste factor for lead. To draw a full-size cutline drawing of the project window use the method described in Section 3.

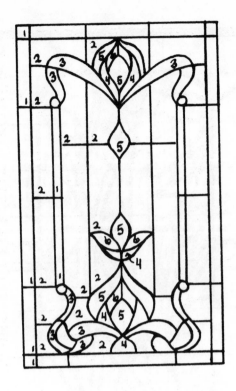

Project: ARABESQUE

Designer: Luciano

Studio: Lucino Stained Glass Art, Palo Alto, Ca.

Dimensions: 18″ × 30″

Section	Color	Type	Amount
1	Purple Blue	Streaky Cathedral	1⅓ sq. ft.
2	Clear	Antique	4 sq. ft.
3	Turquoise	Antique	⅔ sq. ft.
4	Purple	Streaky Antique	⅓ sq. ft.
5	Pink	Streaky Antique	½ sq. ft.
6	Gold	Antique	⅓ sq. ft.
Lead: perimeter		½ ″ round	10 feet
inside		¼ ″ round	38 feet
Solder:		50/50	⅓ pound

Figures for material amounts include a 25% waste factor. The full-size cutline drawing for this window is on side one of the fold out.

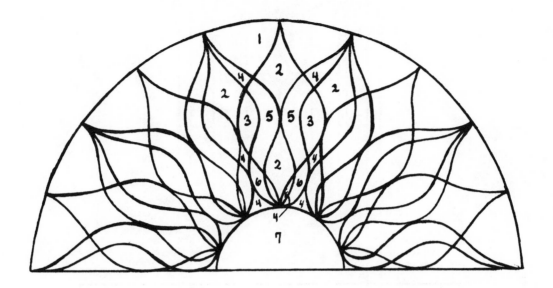

Project: **SUNBURST**

Designer: **Robert W. Hill**

Studio: **Brusey Stained Glass Studio, Soquel, Ca.**

Dimensions: **29″ × 15″**

Section	Color	Type	Amount
1	Blue	Cathedral	2 sq. ft.
2	Deep Olive	Antique	⅔ sq. ft.
3	Light Olive	Antique	⅔ sq. ft.
4	Gold	Antique	½ sq. ft.
5	Orange	Variegated Antique	⅔ sq. ft.
6	Red	Antique	½ sq. ft.
7	Yellow Gold	Blenko	½ sq. ft.
Lead:	perimeter	½ ″ round	14 feet
	inside	¼ ″ round	42 feet
Solder:		50/50	½ pound

Figures for material amounts include a 50% waste factor for glass and a 20% waste factor for lead. A full circle window will require twice the material amounts shown above. The full-size cutline drawing for this window is on side two of the fold out.

Section 20
Project Cutline Drawings

The fold out sheet contains the full-size cutline drawings for the Arabesque and Sunburst windows. The fold out is perforated for easy separation from the book.

The Wonder of Stained Glass
by Luciano & Don Malmstrom

AN INTRODUCTION

The wonder of stained glass, which probably began in the eleventh century, dominated as a church-supported art form in the twelfth and thirteenth centuries in Europe. It was renewed and expanded by the innovations of Louis C. Tiffany and others in the 1890's and now attracts an ever increasing number of artists and home craftsmen.

The purpose of this small book is to share with the thousands of hobbyists who have recently begun to work in the ancient craft, the diverse range of stained glass now available in this country. The color plates contain more than 250 examples of different types and colors of stained glass sheets, jewels, and beveled pieces. Certainly not all the types and color ranges of each manufacturer are represented in our selection. However, you will find among the examples shown many which are readily available from stained glass studios, retail outlets, and national distributors of stained glass supplies.

In addition to this visual introduction to stained glass, brief discussions of the different glassmaking techniques and the names of the major manufacturers are presented. Each maker of stained glass imparts his own artistry to the glass he makes. The differences among and between them are self-evident and important. We hope you will find this "printed pallet" useful when designing your stained glass projects.

TYPES OF STAINED GLASS

There are many different types of glass included in the term Stained Glass, and it is the differences in their respective manufacturing processes that provides the particular characteristics of each type of glass. In the following sections Antique Glass, Cathedral Glass, Opalescent Glass, and Speciality Glass are presented in turn.

Stained glass is composed of silica sand with varying small amounts of iron, limestone, soda ash, and borax. The relative percentage of iron contained in the silica sand is one of the important variants in the glassmaking process. The different colors of stained glass are obtained by the addition of metal oxides to the basic glass materials.*

Blue:	cobalt oxide, and combinations of cobalt and chromium
Red:	selenium in combination with cadmium and copper salts
Red-pink: (Gold-pink)	manganese oxide, gold oxide; this can vary between deep cherry red and light camelia pink; extremely expensive
Purple:	manganese in conjunction with cobalt blue
Yellow:	selenium and chromiun in conjunction with cadmium salts
Sulphur yellow:	sodium
Black:	concentrated copper salts
Green:	copper and chromium salts

Simple single-color glass is known as "pot" glass. The pot, in this case, is the steel-lined vat containing the molten glass from which the blower extracts the glass to be blown. In single-color glass the blower only dips into one pot.

---

*Patrick Reyntiens, *The Technique of Stained Glass*, (New York: Watson-Guptill Publications, 1967), pg. 29.

ANTIQUE GLASS

The term "antique" as used in stained glass refers to the nineteenth century method of making the glass which, with modification, is used by present day manufacturers. It does not mean that the "antique glass" you find in the studios is in fact an "antique," i.e. more than 100 years old. Antique Glass has traditionally been the basic glass of the craftsman.

Antique Sheet Glass (handmade) is mostly blown in elongated cylindrical bubbles approximately 14 inches in diameter and 5 feet in length. As the glass is being blown this bubble is rotated with an up and down motion in a cylindrical trough to achieve even shaping. When the freehand-made glass cylinder is rotated in the V-shaped metal trough, its surface is intentionally scratched by the metal protrusions (spikes) on the trough's inner surface walls. These marks are the manufacturer's fingerprints, and they create the "action" within the glass. This process also imparts the beautiful crystalline surface texture which is characteristic of antique glass. Next, the ends are cut off and the cylinder is split lengthwise down the center with a hot knife or diamond-cut. At this stage the glass is semi-soft and the cylinders are gently flattened out onto a flat sheet. The glass then passes through an annealing oven (for controlled cooling) to remove strains and brittleness. The rate of cooling will vary for each particular glass batch and color depending on the glassmakers' specific technique.

Sheet antique is made by Desag of Germany (see page 5), and typically averages 12 to 13 square feet in area. Glass made in this manner has consistent thickness and even color, with excellent cutting characteristics. Because of these characteristics it is favored by beginning craftsmen. It is available in a wide range of colors. The "action" is missing in some of the photographs due to the technical photographic problems inherent in photographing stained glass.

Full Antique Glass

In making Full Antique Glass the handblown cylindrical bubble is pierced at one end and the edges are fluted into a cylinder. This pierced end is grasped by a metal cage (attached to a pole) and the blow pipe is removed from the other end. The glass is reheated and then this second end is pierced and fluted. The next steps are similar to the general glassmaking technique described for sheet antique. Because full antique is made from smaller bubbles than those used in sheet antique, it has a more uneven thickness, which produces a color shading in the glass ranging from dark to light. Full antique is available in a wide range of colors and is the basis for producing most of the speciality glass described in a later section of this book.

Full antique glass is made by Fisher of Germany (see page 14), Hartley Wood of England (see page 4), St. Gobain of France (see page 4), and Blenko of the United States (see page 12). Blenko glass varies considerably in thickness within a sheet, which produces stunning color variations, but it is somewhat more difficult to cut.

Flashed Antique Glass

Flashed Antique Glass is made by dipping a large bubble of a base color (usually the lighter of the two colors) into a pot of some darker (and super-heated) color. The coated bubble is mouth-blown and made in the same manner as the previously discussed antique glass. The resultant glass has a thin layer of strong color on top of a thicker layer of the base color. Reds, greens, and blues are often flashed glass. Flashed glass is often used by the craftsman to add surface art work to it either by sandblasting, engraving, or acid etching methods (these are discussed later).

The oval on page 18 is an example of a St. Gobain flashed glass (red or gold) with the gold flower produced by engraving. For other examples see pages 4, 14, and 24. Semi-Antique Glass is machine made antique (imitation German antique) by Desag and St. Gobain (imitation French antique). The German glass has vertical striations and the French glass has wide, sweeping "action" curves. The machine-made antique is produced by the vertical draw or Fourcault method. The striations (or action pattern) are transferred to the glass as it is drawn over the first roller. The machine-made glass is of even thickness with consistent color and high brilliance. It is produced in clear (no color) and light tints of grey, blue, amber, green, and flesh tone. It is less expensive than antique glass and is often used for backgrounds in windows.

2

English Opalescent Transluscent

English Opalescent Transluscent

Purple Streaky Full Antique

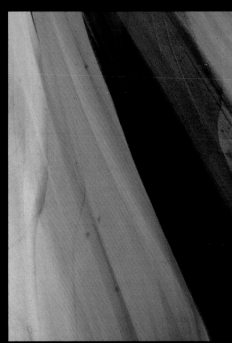

Full Antique Gold Pink Streaky

Streaky Antique

Streaky Antique Glass is made similar to flashed glass except in this instance the base bubble of glass is not completely coated by the overlaying color (or colors). Instead the color(s) used in coating is intertwined and swirled about the base color. The front cover shows a multi-colored streaky and the back cover another streaky, both of which are examples of glass by Fisher of Germany (see page 13). You will find examples of other streaky antique glass by Hartley Wood (see pages 3 and 4) and St. Gobain (see page 24). Streaky glass is one of the more difficult glasses to cut.

3

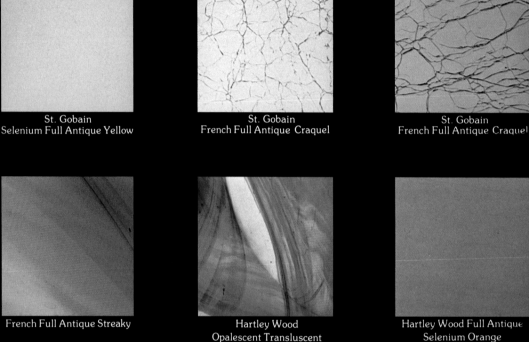

St. Gobain
Flashed

St. Gobain
French Full Antique

St. Gobain
French Full Antique Craquel

St. Gobain
Selenium Full Antique Yellow

St. Gobain
French Full Antique Craquel

St. Gobain
French Full Antique Craquel

French Full Antique Streaky

Hartley Wood
Opalescent Transluscent

Hartley Wood Full Antique
Selenium Orange

Hartley Wood Full Antique

Advance Sales Cathedral

Advance Sales
Star Pattern Cathedral

Reamy Antique

This glass is a light variant of streaky. Much lighter in tone and color, it permits a greater
amount of light to pass through. This glass has heavy cords and mottled areas of extra surface
materials, which lends it a very primitive, handmade appearance. It is available in clear, light
ambers, browns, off whites, greens, and light blues. It may also contain seeds of light, of
heavy and medium density. Seeds are the air bubbles intentionally suspended in the glass. You
will find examples of seedy glass on pages 7, 9, and 10.

Bulls Eye Cats Paw
Opalescent

Bulls Eye Confetti

Bulls Eye Confetti

Bulls Eye Cats Paw
Opalescent

Bulls Eye Confetti

Desag Antique

Desag Antique

Desag Antique

Desag Antique

Desag Antique

Desag Antique

Desag Antique

Desag Antique

Desag Antique

Craguel Antique

This antique glass, when in the molten state, is quickly immersed in water. This is done prior to blowing the glass. Only the outside surface is cooled (not the core of the glass bubble). This process results in the cragueled effect shown on page 4. The sheets may have a large or fine cragueled effect. This will vary depending upon the manufacturer.

CATHEDRAL GLASS

Cathedral Glass is typically glass that has been "double-rolled" by machine. The rollers of the machine may be embossed with a texture which is impressed on the glass sheet. Because this glass is machine rolled it has even thickness, consistent color, and is fairly easy to cut. Cathedral glass is single-color (monochromatic) and does not quite have the brilliance and trueness of handblown antique glass. But it is less expensive. The glass is made by melting

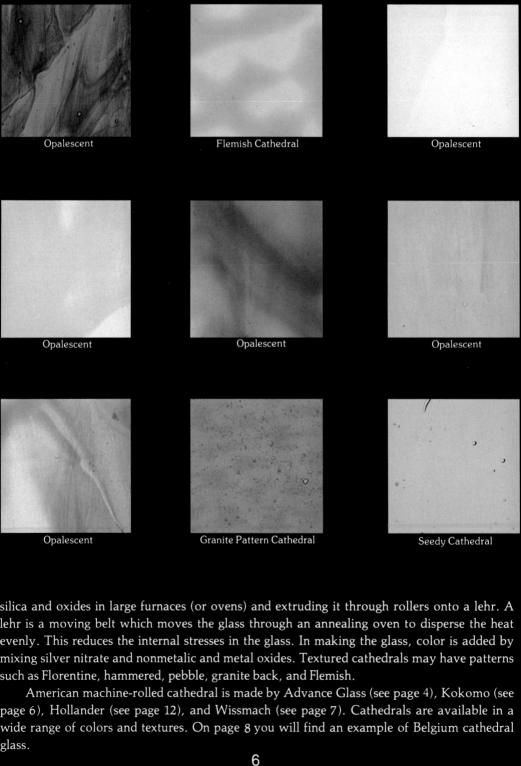

Cathedral

Opalescent

Opalescent

Opalescent

Flemish Cathedral

Opalescent

Opalescent

Opalescent

Opalescent

Opalescent

Granite Pattern Cathedral

Seedy Cathedral

silica and oxides in large furnaces (or ovens) and extruding it through rollers onto a lehr. A lehr is a moving belt which moves the glass through an annealing oven to disperse the heat evenly. This reduces the internal stresses in the glass. In making the glass, color is added by mixing silver nitrate and nonmetalic and metal oxides. Textured cathedrals may have patterns such as Florentine, hammered, pebble, granite back, and Flemish.

American machine-rolled cathedral is made by Advance Glass (see page 4), Kokomo (see page 6), Hollander (see page 12), and Wissmach (see page 7). Cathedrals are available in a wide range of colors and textures. On page 8 you will find an example of Belgium cathedral glass.

6

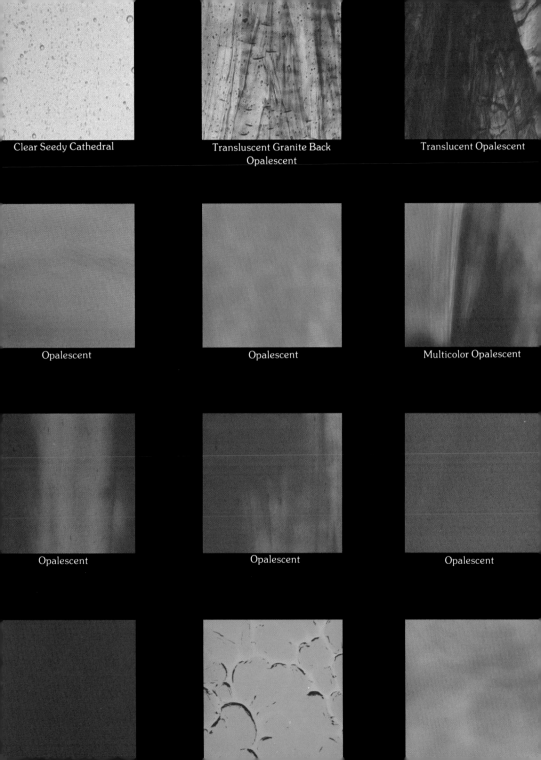

Clear Seedy Cathedral

Transluscent Granite Back
Opalescent

Translucent Opalescent

Opalescent

Opalescent

Multicolor Opalescent

Opalescent

Opalescent

Opalescent

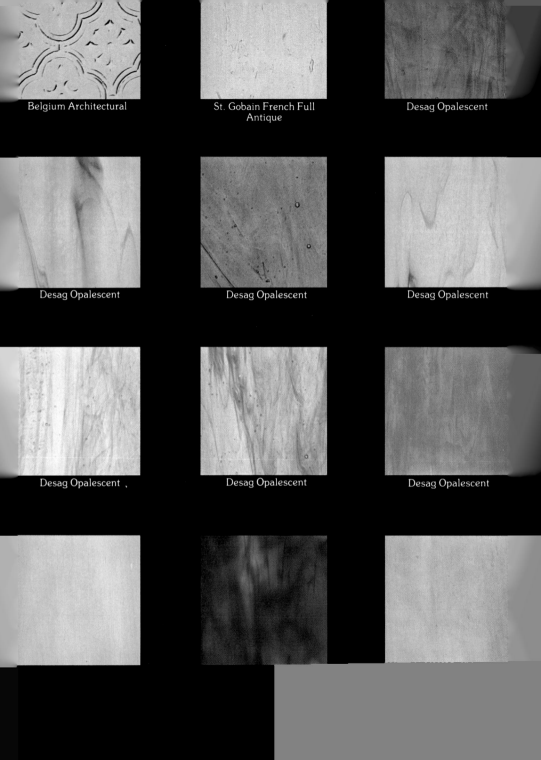

Belgium Architectural

St. Gobain French Full Antique

Desag Opalescent

Desag Opalescent

Desag Opalescent

Desag Opalescent

Desag Opalescent

Desag Opalescent

Desag Opalescent

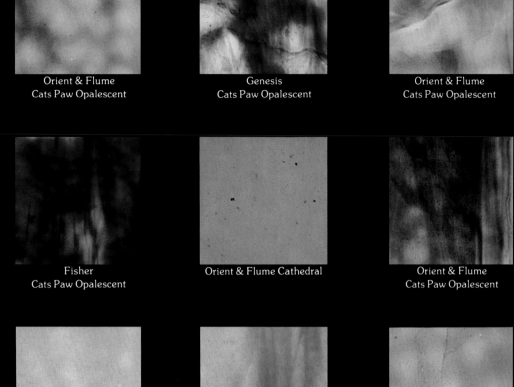

Orient & Flume Cats Paw Opalescent	Genesis Cats Paw Opalescent	Orient & Flume Cats Paw Opalescent
Fisher Cats Paw Opalescent	Orient & Flume Cathedral	Orient & Flume Cats Paw Opalescent
Orient & Flume Cats Paw Opalescent	Genesis Cats Paw Opalescent	Orient & Flume Cats Paw Opalescent
Kokomo Cathedral Seedy	Wismark Cathedral	Wismach Cathedral Hammered

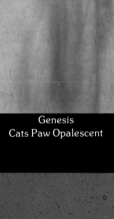

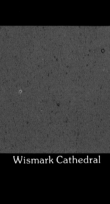

Opalescents are domestically manufactured by Advance Glass, Kokomo (see page 6), Scott (see page 15), Spectrum (see page 10), Wissmach (see page 7), and Wheaton Industries (see page 11). You will find an example of Hartley Wood opalescent translucent on page 4, and a Desag opalescent on page 8.

Cats Paw Opals

This type of opal has a mottled effect, i.e. "cats paw," which is achieved by a reheating of the glass in the first chamber of the lehr. When hot glass is rolled over a cool cast iron plate it starts to contract immediately. This creates a bumpy surface where the sheet touches the plate. You will find examples of cats paw as follows: Bulls Eye, page 5; Orient & Flume, page 9; Fisher, page 14 .

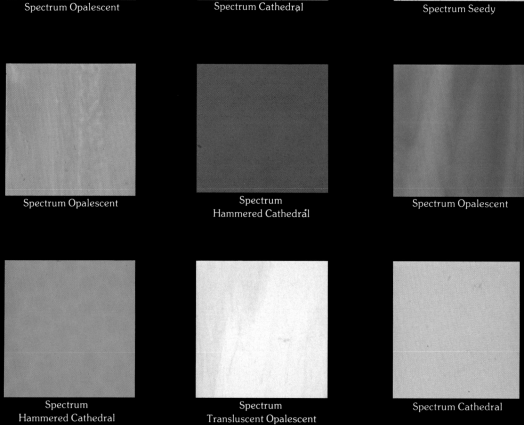

Spectrum Opalescent

Spectrum Cathedral

Spectrum Seedy

Spectrum Opalescent

Spectrum
Hammered Cathedral

Spectrum Opalescent

Spectrum
Hammered Cathedral

Spectrum
Transluscent Opalescent

Spectrum Cathedral

Spectrum Seedy Cathedral

Genesis Ripple Cathedral

Genesis Ripple Cathedral

Opaque Opal

This is a flashed opal with a muted (milky) finish to the glass. It is made by Fisher (see page 14), Lamber, and Wheaton Industries (see page 11).

Feather Glass (Glue Chip Glass)

This is a cathedral glass produced by sandblasting the surface of the glass and then applying a layer of hoof and horn animal glue (or first glue). The treated sheet is then placed in dryer ovens (or racks). As the glue drys it shrinks and contracts, pulling sections out of the glass surface. The result is a fern or feather pattern with slightly irregular sandblasted areas. Glass with one application of glue is known as single-chip, and glass which has undergone two applications is known as double-chip. Double-chip glass has a more crystalline surface. Feather glass was used a great deal in the Victorian era. It is now available in a moderate range of colors.

10

Feather

Feather

Feather

Feather

Feather

Feather

Hartley Wood
Gold Pink Streaky

Feather Snail Chip

Feather

Wheaton
Cats Paw Opalescent

Wheaton Translucent

Wheaton Heavy Opaque

Domestic manufacturers of this glass are H and N Specialties, Hollander Glass, New Renaissance Glass, and Art Glass of Colorado. The glass is available in ambers, blues, clear, rose, burgundy, reds and greens (see page 11).

Special Glass

In addition to the above general types of glass, various manufacturers make available specialty glass such as confetti glass (see page 5), iridescent glass, and ripple glass (see pages 10 and 14). Glass produced as one-of-a-kind runs that don't fit into regular production categories are called "curious" glass.

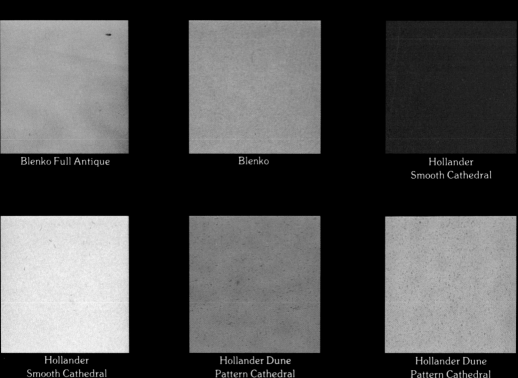

| Blenko | Blenko Full Antique | Blenko |

| Blenko Full Antique | Blenko | Hollander Smooth Cathedral |

| Hollander Smooth Cathedral | Hollander Dune Pattern Cathedral | Hollander Dune Pattern Cathedral |

| Hollander Smooth Cathedral | Hollander Smooth Cathedral | Hollander Smooth Cathedral |

BEVELED GLASS

The special effects of Beveled Glass are shown on pages 15 and 16. The beveled edges cause light to refract into a rainbow of colors. Additional special treatments of beveled glass include engraving, etching, silk screening, and sandblasting designs on the flat surface of the beveled piece. These special treatments are discussed in the following sections.

Hand Processed Bevels

To shape bevels by hand is a time consuming process which requires patience, experience, and practiced skills. In general, 1/4-inch or 3/16-inch thick plate glass is used. The craftsman first cuts the plate glass to the desired shape and grinds and polishes about 1/2-inch of the perimeter. The resultant angle (bevel) should be uniform, without scratches, waves, or processing marks.

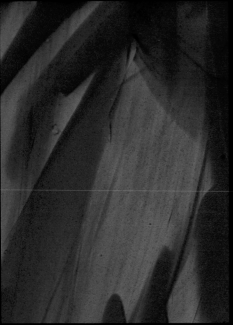

Fisher Streaky German Full Antique

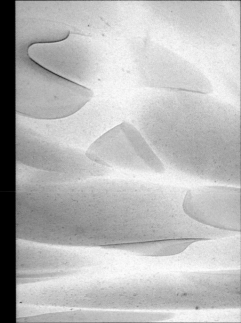

Fisher Streaky German Full Antique

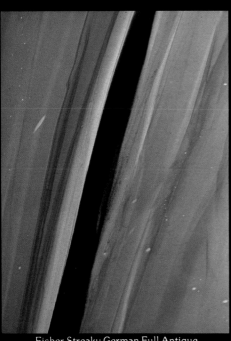

Fisher Streaky German Full Antique

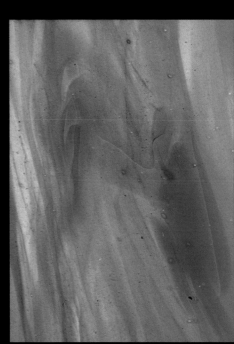

Fisher Streaky German Full Antique

In the first step of the beveling process a roughing plate (large 2 1/2-inch diameter stone wheel, motor driven) is used to create the desired angle along the edges of the glass, reducing the edges to the desired thickness to fit into the lead came. Next, a smoothing plate (2 1/2-inch diameter smoother stone, motor driven) is used to clear the beveled areas of rough surface caused by the roughing plate. Polishing is first begun using a motor driven cork wheel and pumice powder. The final polishing involves the use of a felt wheel covered with serium oxide powder. A unique example of a custom jewel created by this process is shown on page 22. It was designed using a piece of 1-inch thick dalle glass by Mark Walton, of Walton Studios. Hand beveling is most often used in custom work and provides the flexibility needed to bevel pieces with inside and outside curves.

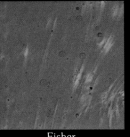
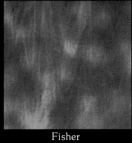

Fisher
Cats Paw Opalescent

Fisher
Cats Paw Opalescent

Fisher
Cats Paw Opalescent

Fisher Streaky

Fisher Multicolored
Streaky

Fisher Streaky

Fisher Opaque

Fisher Antique

Fisher Craquel Flashed

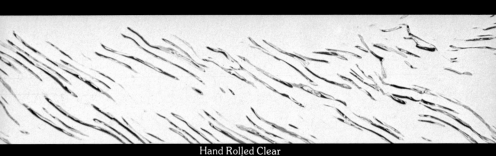

Hand Rolled Clear
Ripple by David Ruth

Most bevel processing setups are designed and custom made to fit the needs of each individual studio. Quarries, which in the past provided the stones for making roughing and smoothing plates, are almost gone, so there now exists a limited quantity of the required beveling wheels.

Machine Processed Bevels

Machine beveling is accomplished by the use of diamonds to grind (bevel) the edge of the glass in one step. Other machines are then used to smooth and polish the beveled surfaces. Mass produced bevels are generally 3/16-inch thick, although the manufacturers have recently been changing over to the use of 1/4-inch thick plate. Machine processed bevels may not be of the same quality as those of hand-processed bevels, but their lower price and uniformity are attractive features. Generally, machine processing has less flexibility in treating inside and outside curves and small pieces.

14

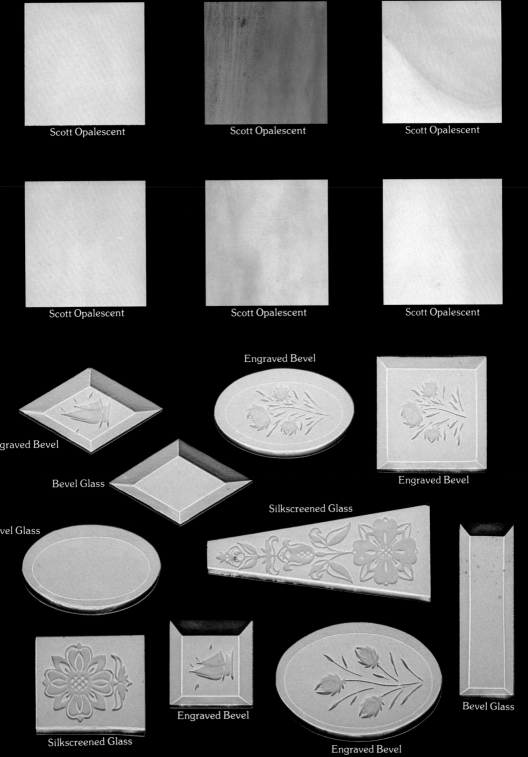

Scott Opalescent

Scott Opalescent

Scott Opalescent

Scott Opalescent

Scott Opalescent

Scott Opalescent

Engraved Bevel

graved Bevel

Bevel Glass

Engraved Bevel

vel Glass

Silkscreened Glass

Silkscreened Glass

Engraved Bevel

Engraved Bevel

Bevel Glass

Beveled pieces are often used as borders in stained glass windows, as well as in "French Doors." You may find large lamps with a skirt formed completely of bevels.

JEWELS AND OTHER THREE DIMENSIONAL SHAPES

Hand cut jewels are quite rare. Luckily, machine processed jewels are common and are still being manufactured. Because of the improved quality of present day stained glass techniques, the new jewels being made in Austria, Czechoslovakia, Germany, and the United States are brighter, more uniform, and offer a greater range of colors than the "antique" jewels. On pages 17 through 23 you will find more than 90 examples of present day and "antique" (old) jewels.

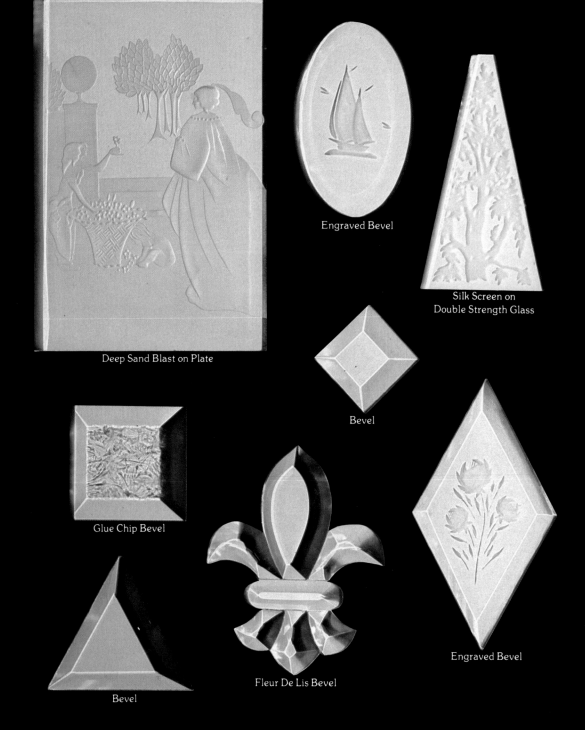

Engraved Bevel

Silk Screen on
Double Strength Glass

Deep Sand Blast on Plate

Bevel

Glue Chip Bevel

Engraved Bevel

Bevel

Fleur De Lis Bevel

Machine Processed Jewels

Jewels are made using a solid glass rod of a specified color. One end of the rod is heated to a
molten state in a furnace and then inserted in a mold. A plunger is used to accomplish this. If
the plunger has a design the resultant jewel is two-sided. If not, the mold has the design and
the jewel is one-sided. The other side is flat-surfaced. The jewels are pressed out, then placed
on a lehr to slowly cool. After cooling the flat side (of one-sided jewels), they are machine
polished. The faceted side of the jewels does not usually require polishing

Opalescent Rondell

"Antique"

"Antique"

Hand Painted
Jewel

Blob

Other Shapes

Squares made similar to rondels are also available in various shapes, textures, and sizes. The one shown in the upper left-hand corner on page 20 is believed to be a quite old handmade square jewel. The one shown on page 22 was crimped, causing a shading in the color intensity as light passes through it.

Blobs or globs (see page 21) are humps of glass varying in color and shape; they are made in free-form fashion in a kiln. They have a flat surface on the back side and may be integrated by foiling or leading in the window or lamp design. They may also be glued to the surface of a stained glass design.

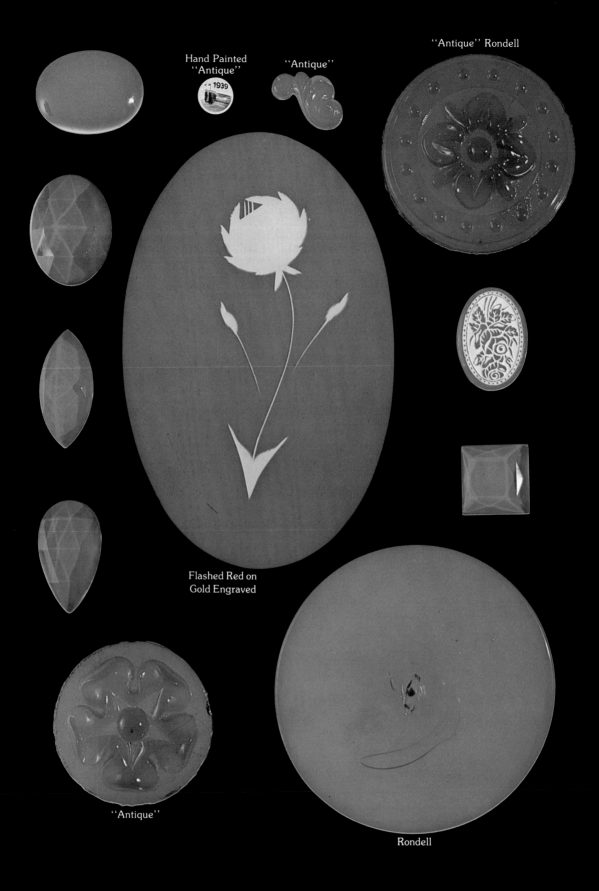

Hand Painted
"Antique"

"Antique"

"Antique" Rondell

Flashed Red on
Gold Engraved

"Antique"

Rondell

Most jewels are translucent. Special treatments include chemically etched designs. Hand painted jewels are rare. Those shown in this book may have come from the 1939 Expositions in New York and San Francisco. The cameo shown on page 19 is the result of combining a chemically etched design with a vacuum-plated, copper-backed surface. Jewels may be integrated in window designs for highlighting, and are particularly effective in stained glass lamps.

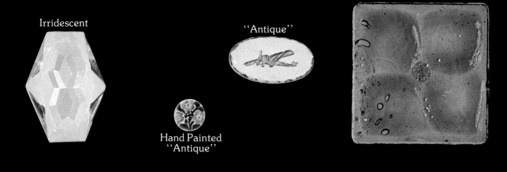

Irridescent

"Antique"

Hand Painted
"Antique"

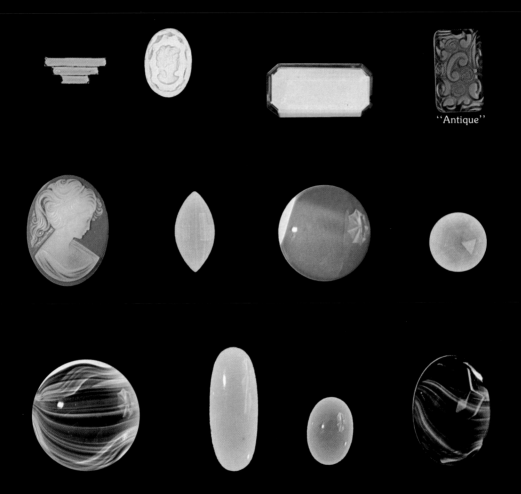

"Antique"

Rondel

Rondels are spun glass circles either handmade or machine pressed. They are generally made using translucent glass but opalescent glass may also be used (see page 22). Machine pressed rondels may further be enhanced with surface designs and raised textures for special effects (see page 21). They will range in size from 1 inches to 12 inches and can usually be found in reds, oranges, yellows, and greens. Used sparingly in a window they add dramatic impact. The smallest of the rondels are suitable for repeated geometric designs within a lamp.

SPECIAL SURFACE TREATMENTS

In this section a brief description of special surface treatments to glass is presented. Some professionals classify the following three types, silk screening on glass, sandblasting glass, and engraving glass, as "etching." Each of the three processes yields unique design characteristics to the glass.

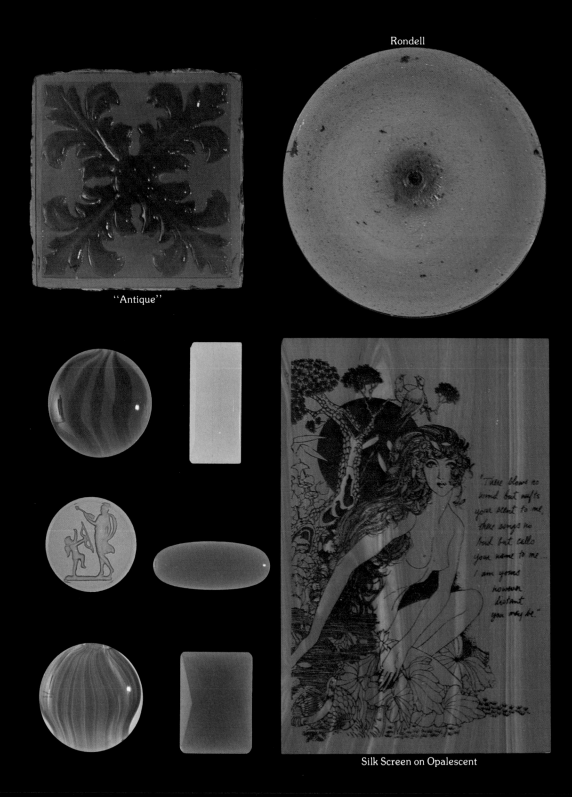

Rondell

"Antique"

Silk Screen on Opalescent

Sandblasting

In general, sandblasting is the pitting of the top surface of the glass by the use of various grades of sand directed at glass under pressure (using an air compressor). A stencil is used, which exposes the areas of the glass to be sandblasted. Various depths and textures can be achieved through the use of assorted course and fine grain sands. You are familiar with the effect of the glass design appearing as "frosted." An example of a deep sandblasted design on plate glass is shown on page 16.

The design is transferred to stencil material (some craftsmen use contact paper) and the areas of the design to be treated are cut from the stencil exposing the top surface of the glass. Sandblasting can be used effectively on clear, plate, mirror plate, double-strength, and flashed

"Antique"

"Antique"

Hand Painted
"Antique"

Blob

Special Effect Rondell

"Antique"

glass. A treatment, sometimes called "carving" is used to deeply etch the glass. This is done by sandblasting in order to produce shadings within the design, in effect creating a textured base relief. Some glass studios as well as professional sandblasting companies will sandblast the glass to your designs.

Wheel Engraving

Engraving glass is a more expensive process than sandblasting. Glass engravers are true specialists with finely honed skills. Generally the design is engraved in the transparent glass by

21

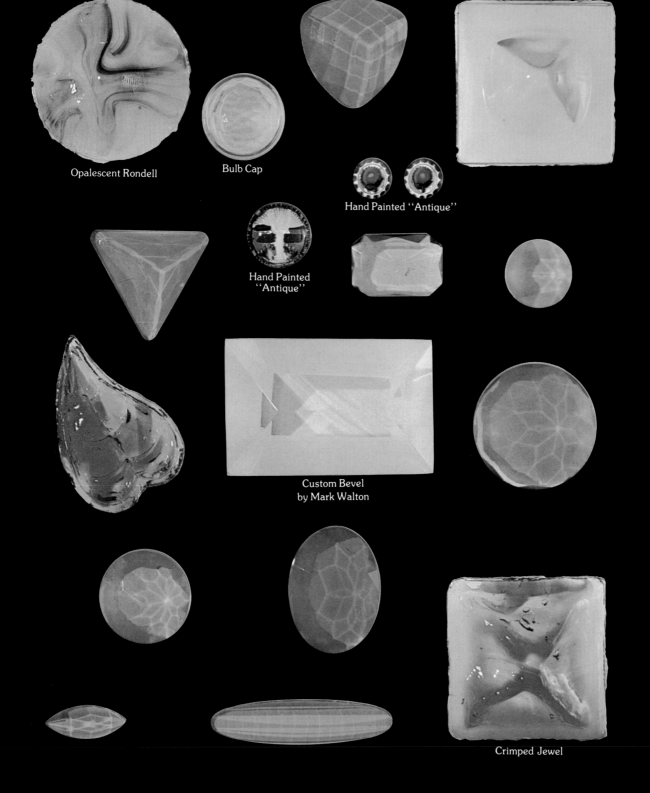

Opalescent Rondell

Bulb Cap

Hand Painted "Antique"

Hand Painted "Antique"

Custom Bevel
by Mark Walton

Crimped Jewel

scratching the bottom surface (usually) with a variable speed stone lathe. Wheels of various sizes and shapes are used. The wheels may be made of sandstone, aluminum, oxide, or silicon carbide. The engraver also shapes his stone wheels to most effectively achieve the desired design effect. This shaping of the stone is known as "dressing the stone." The engraved area appears frosted. If the engraved design is to be transparent, the engraver will then use a cork polishing wheel with jewelers' rough and pumice powder. You will find an example of engraved design or flashed glass in the oval on the front cover, and examples of engraved beveled designs on pages 15 and 16.

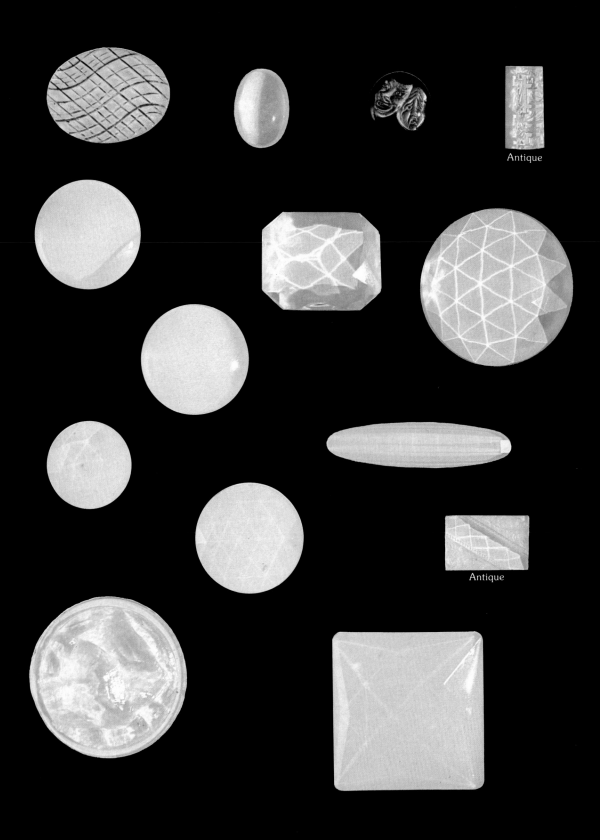

Antique

Antique

Silk Screening

Silk screening is the process by which a design is etched on the glass surface using an etching cream (or hydrofluoric acid), which passes through the design made on the silk screen (nylon mesh). The cream is both safer and easier to use than the acid. The design is first transferred photographically to the silk screen. Then the null areas of the design (those not to be etched on the glass) are masked. The warmed cream then is applied to the silk screen and passes through

23

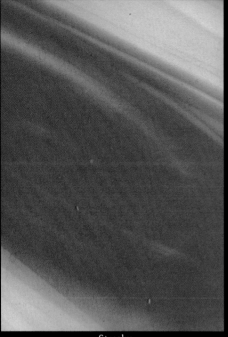

Streaky

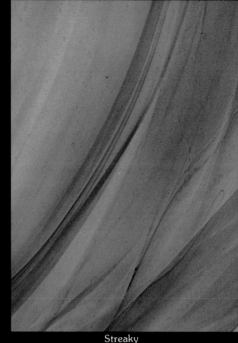

Streaky

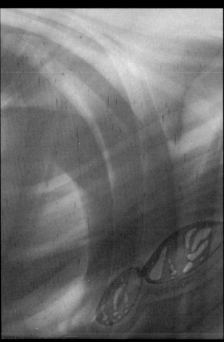

Streaky

Flashed Red on Blue

the now masked areas on to the glass. The silk screen is removed and after a three-or four-minute wait, the cream is rinsed from the glass. You can repeat the process hundreds of times using the same silk screen; therefore, it's an excellent production process.

Silk screening can be used on nearly any type of glass. An example of its use on opalescent glass is shown on page 20, on cathedral glass on page 17, and on beveled glass and double-strength glass on pages 15 and 16.

Sandblasting, engraving, and silk screening provide a great deal of design flexability, and when appropriately integrated into your project they will greatly enhance its dramatic impact.

Sunburst
by
Robert W. Hill
29" x 15"